THE SPIRIT WORLD IN PLAIN ENGLISH

Books by Glyn Edwards and Santoshan

Glyn Edwards, with an introduction by Santoshan
The Potential of Mediumship: A Collection of Essential Teachings and Exercises

Glyn Edwards and Santoshan
*Spirit Gems: Essential Guidance for Spiritual, Mediumistic and Creative
Unfoldment* (revised and expanded edition of *Unleash your Spiritual Power and Grow*
– first published as *21 Steps to Reach your Spirit*)

Swami Dharmananda and Santoshan, with a foreword by Glyn Edwards
The House of Wisdom: Yoga Spirituality of the East and West

Santoshan, with conversations with Glyn Edwards
*Realms of Wondrous Gifts: Psychic, Mediumistic and Miraculous Powers in the Great
Mystical and Wisdom Traditions*

Santoshan, with a foreword by Ian Mowll
Spirituality Unveiled: Awakening to Creative Life

Santoshan
*Rivers of Green Wisdom: Exploring Christian and Yogic Earth
Centred Spirituality*

Edited by Santoshan (multi-authored)
*Pathways of Green Wisdom: Discovering Earth Centred Teachings in
Spirituality and Religious Traditions*

THE Spirit World
in plain English

Mediumistic and
Spiritual Unfoldment

Glyn Edwards & Santoshan

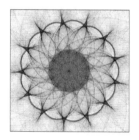

Foreword by Don Hills

Published by
S Wollaston, 2011
Publishing address: 33 Cobden Road, London E11 3PE

For Retail Orders and Wholesale Information Contact:
Mind-Body-Spirit
Telephone: (01202) 267684 / International: +441202 267684
Email: info@mindbodyspirit-uk.com
Website: www.mindbodyspiritonline.co.uk

ISBN: 978-0-9569210-0-0

A CIP record of this book is available from the British Library

The Spirit World in Plain English is a revised and updated edition of
Tune in to your Spiritual Potential
First published by Quantum, an imprint of W Foulsham, in 1999

Design and artwork: Santoshan (Stephen Wollaston)
Cover image: © Alexnika/Shutterstock.com

Printed and bound by CPI Group (UK), Croydon, CR0 4YY

Printed on FSC accredited paper

Contents

*G*lyn Edwards is internationally recognized as one of the UK's greatest mediums and teachers of spiritual and psychic science. At sixteen he joined a Benedictine community. He later became a protégée of the medium, Gordon M Higginson, and founded the Gordon Higginson Awareness Foundation. He has been a regular and highly popular senior course tutor at the esteemed Arthur Findlay College for over three decades and has run workshops and demonstrated his mediumship throughout the world. He is a certificate holder of the Spiritualist' National Union, has coauthored books, recorded various teaching CDs and cassettes and was given the name Devadasa (servant of God) by Swami Dharmananda Saraswati Maharaj. He is particularly known for the quality of his teaching and his ability to demonstrate his mediumship almost effortlessly in front of large audiences.

*S*antoshan (Stephen Wollaston) has served as a council member of GreenSpirit, is a member of their editorial and publishing team and the designer of GreenSpirit Magazine. He was given the name Santoshan (contentment) by Swami Dharmananda and has a creative background as a writer, graphic designer, artist and musician. He was the bass guitarist of one of London's first punk rock bands, The Wasps, and is the author and coauthor of several acclaimed books, including *Spirituality Unveiled: Awakening to Creative Life* and *The House of Wisdom: Yoga Spirituality of the East and West* (coauthored). He holds a degree in religious studies and a post graduate certificate in religious education from King's College London and studied psychosynthesis psychology. He also helped to establish a spiritual organization that ran various courses with Glyn Edwards, and has a deep interest in creative, Yogic and Nature centred spiritualities.

Dedicated to
Eileen Davies, Jean Dixon and Mark Stone

Foreword

By Don Hills

I have been on the track of Earth-based spirituality for the past 10 plus years and so it came as a surprise to find myself in the worlds of psychic awareness, auras, mediumistic unfoldment and powers, trance and physical mediumship. Yet nowhere did I feel out of my depth spiritually, and this was I think because Glyn and Santoshan emphasize that all forms of spiritual expression need balance, breadth and the wisdom brought by allying common sense with compassion. For them, all realms of development, including mediumistic unfoldment, imply honouring the laws of Nature and a spiritual way of life and living. Here is a typical passage from page 96:

Ultimately, as with all people following spiritual paths, mediums will need to consider how to unfold and develop a closer union with the Divine, with Nature and all of humankind. They will need to embrace ways in which to awaken within themselves a deeper creativity and appreciation of the awe inspiring evolving universe in which we live. This includes awakening to the Earth's natural beauty and to realms of love and wisdom, as this will cultivate mediums' minds and characters.

Their book is very strong on the virtues of meditation, silence, attentiveness and concentration – things very dear to myself. So when it came to setting out, for example, the principles of effective mediumship, their explanations were clothed in terms I could readily empathise with. Similarly with the phenomenon of trance in all of its fascinating forms – for them this is, "a means by which the spirit can influence and awaken within the medium the ability to become a finer instrument for the dissemination of spiritual wisdom."

For me, perhaps the strongest feature of this book, is the

emphasis on practical spirituality. It is crammed with suggested exercises and guidelines for practice. Indeed, in the Preface, the authors describe *The Spirit World in Plain English* as, "essentially a workbook for those who wish to embrace the *all-ness* of mediumistic and spiritual growth." They are at pains to make clear what the "various exercises and practices are useful for, and what may or may not be expected through practising them."

With all of this in mind, I heartily recommend this deeply spiritual book for its evident breadth and depth of vision and relevance to our troubled times.

Preface

*T*he *Spirit World in Plain English* is organised in three parts. Part One, *Ways*, gives guidance on various practices for travellers on spiritual paths. Part Two, *Attunement*, focuses on psychic and mediumistic abilities and is intended to give readers a practical understanding of these powers and how to unfold them. Part Three, *Synthesis*, looks at individual development and what is needed for living a balanced life. At the end of each part there are various exercises. There are also ones included in the chapters. For exercises that have various sections to them, you may like to ask a friend to lead you through them or record yourself reading them and meditate to your recording. Be sure to leave an appropriate length of space between the different sections if you do this.

The Spirit World in Plain English is essentially a workbook for those who wish to embrace the *all-ness* of mediumistic and spiritual growth. Numerous insights are shared in order to make it clear what various exercises and practices are useful for, and what may or may not be expected through practising them.

It should be mentioned that where the word 'spirit' appears with a small 's' it refers to one's inner spirit or to individual spirit helpers and the world they inhabit. Spirit in this sense may be referred to in the plural (one often hears mediums talk of 'the *spirit* and *their* influence'). Where a capital 'S' is used, it refers to the *supreme Spirit* and represents a single reality. Similarly, 'Self' may be written with a capital 'S' to denote the *higher spiritual Self* or with a small 's' to denote the *individual psychological self*.

Acknowledgements

I wish to give a personal thanks to Santoshan for his involvement in revising, updating and redesigning this book. His writing and designing skills have brought a new freshness, clarity and more contemporary feel to its overall contents that have amazingly made it read and look almost like a whole new book. For me the words shine through so much brighter than ever before because of his involvement and the new title highlights what we were both aiming to achieve. Santoshan's insights into creativity and how it interacts with the continuous creativity of God and Nature, also highlight important areas connected with the spirit.

I also wish to thank numerous students and working colleagues for requesting the book's re-release (published previously under the title *Tune in to your Spiritual Potential*). Without their enthusiasm about its contents, this new revised edition would not have been thought of and would never have come into being.

– GLYN EDWARDS

*L*ike many people I have been privileged to meet and make friends with numerous inspiring and encouraging teachers, come across amazing insightful writers who struck deep chords within me, experienced unexpected intervention from the spirit world in a time of great need and stood amidst the astounding beauty of Nature and been uplifted by her awe inspiring creative work. It is to all these companions, including Sri Jammu Maharaj, Swami Dharmananda Saraswati, Bhikkhu Nagasena, the healer, medium and saxophonist, Bob Bassett, and to Mother Earth herself that I wish to give my sincerest thanks. Without them my part in this book would not have been possible.

13

I must also give thanks to coauthor Glyn Edwards, who has been a close friend for over twenty years. In the course of this time Glyn has often nudged me to look deeper into areas I was sometimes only skimming, but later I would realise he had been right to draw these things to my attention. He has even helped to fund this updated edition, for which I am most grateful. It is not often I get the chance to revisit something I had previously been involved in writing and apply new insights. Working with Glyn again on the following chapters has given me this unique opportunity.

– Santoshan (Stephen Wollaston)

Introduction

The Spirit World in Plain English is a compilation of shared thoughts, observations, experiences and practices Santoshan and I have found useful in our own search and unfoldment. Like any two authors, we come from slightly different backgrounds. But we also share vast areas of common ground. This was how we were able to work so closely together on many chapters.

The motive behind writing the following pages was not to add more *concepts* to people's knowledge of mediumship and spirituality, but to serve as a practical guide to various aspects of unfoldment which will, I hope, help readers in their quests to become more receptive to the wholeness of growth and unfold numerous gifts that interconnect with the spirit.

In approaching mediumistic and spiritual unfoldment, there are no set rules to follow to reach a specific goal. There are only guidelines and pointers that can be offered. It is up to each of us to decide which roads we wish to take that are best suited to our nature. Ultimately, mediumistic and spiritual unfoldment are active and evolving paths that lead to new and profound experience and deep communion with the world of the spirit.

Those who are open and inclusive in the paths they tread, will find more areas of their lives receptive to unfoldment and will take part in the spirit's work in more fruitful ways. The time to start out on this quest is now, as the present holds many possibilities. All we need to do is be responsive to positive growth and willing to be more active instruments for the compassionate and creative work of the spirit.

– GLYN EDWARDS

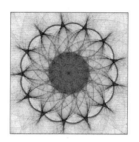

Part 1

Ways

Be mindful, open and compassionate.

Word Power

Lead me from the visible to the invisible.
Take me from the shadow into light.
Teach me how to attune my life with the spirit.

We should not underestimate the power of words in our development, as language is one of the most powerful gifts that we have. Words have the capacity to express our innermost feelings: they can unite or divide nations and express pure unconditional love, or hatred and bitterness. If one person were to speak harshly to another, the abused person might feel a sense of outrage at being treated unjustly and his or her emotions would suddenly change – even if only one harsh word were spoken. So if just one word can have such an adverse effect and give rise to negative emotions, we must also consider what use words can have for positive use and growth.

It is no coincidence that the many spiritual traditions of the world have adopted various uses of prayers, chants, mantras and affirmations. Each can affect and help us in different ways; each have their own value if used correctly. They all provide ways of transcending everything that denies the spirit that we are, so that we centre our awareness in the truth of our being. As we pray or chant, we reflect on God and the spirit world and eventually become absorbed in their presence.

The psychology of chants, mantras and affirmations
In the far east, chants and mantras have long been recognized as important aids in spiritual development. In fact, every word we use and every thought we have is a kind of mantra. We are constantly feeding our unconscious mind with words and thoughts that produce different results, as our conscious mind affects the unconscious level of our being, and our unconscious mind affects the conscious level of our being. We might pay little attention to something and have little attachment to it. Therefore, it will have little hold over us. On the other hand, we may have an experience to which we react quite strongly

and negatively. In this case, it can have a lasting effect upon us. But as explained above, it is not just at the conscious level that we are affected, as every experience is recorded by our unconscious mind, which in turn influences the conscious mind. It is a never-ending cycle, which if we are not careful, can become more and more negative and lead us further away from awakening to our spiritual consciousness. The more negative experiences we feed in, the more negative our character can become, and the more negative our reactions can be. Yet if we keep the conscious mind actively focused upon the positive nature of God and spirit whilst praying, chanting or using an affirmation, we can start to transform our individual nature and draw strength from the infinite creative Source of all.

The power of chants, mantras and affirmations

Chants, mantras and affirmations give us a tool to change our level of awareness in skilful ways. They help us stop our conscious minds behaving so erratically. They also help us to keep our minds focused upon an aspect of our true nature and cease the flow of negative reactions, so that we become more positive and attract and develop attributes connected to richer levels of being. Thus we use the law of cause and effect wholesomely to enhance our spiritual potential.

Chants and mantras have meaning as well as purpose. They are not merely abstract sounds. The mantra So Ham (pronounced Sah-Hum) means 'I Am That'. Om (pronounced O-aum) is said to be the first sound that God created, from which all else was made. Therefore, if you meditate on So Ham – which is practised by 'silently' repeating So on the in-breath and Ham on the out-breath – you will be meditating on the God within. If you chant Om, you meditate on a sound that is said to have created all life and to resonate throughout the universe: "In the beginning was the Word, and the Word was with God, and the Word was God", John's Gospel tells us.[1] Interestingly, some eastern mystics are said to have heard the sound of Om in certain states of meditation.

Most mantras are positive statements that either affirm or surrender to God's presence. Others represent vital sounds that vibrate within us and the universe. If we wish to achieve benefit from these practices, we need to be aware of their purpose and conscious of their particular sound and vibration resonating within ourselves as we use them.

Some might feel uncomfortable using a language or tradition different from their own and will be more at ease repeating the word *God* on the in- or out-breath, and through this focus their attention upon the Divine within. Others may find a phrase or sentence in their own language more helpful. There are of course many types of chants, mantras and affirmations. Each serves a different purpose. You might wish to try using a word that has a quality you are hoping to unfold, or use an affirmation that is more descriptive in helping you to recognize the spirit that you are. All can be of benefit in your development.

Affirmations for use on your spiritual journey

The following affirmations can be used in meditation or during your normal day. But do not repeat them at times when you should be giving your full attention to something else, such as driving a car or operating machinery:

I surrender to the spirit of the inner Self.

The spirit's direction is my direction.

I honour the supreme Spirit in all life.

Using mantras

When you use a word or phrase in a repeated mantra form, create a rhythm between the word(s) and your breathing – repeating it (them) once for every in- and out-breath. Breathe calmly and evenly and repeat the word(s). First voice the mantra for a period of time to get used to the way it sounds. After a while, repeat it silently, taking the sound and rhythm of the mantra within yourself. If you use one of the traditional yogic or Buddhist mantras, it is important to get the correct pronunciation and sound of the mantra, so that it resonates properly within you.

When choosing a specific mantra as your main one (others can be used and changed as secondary mantras), it is advised that you retain it for use over a period of time – some say for life. Do not change it from week to week, but use the same one regularly in order to gain full benefit from it. Unlike some methods of meditation where a word that has a passive quality about it, such as 'peace', can be reflected upon, it is better to use something more specific that invokes the universal creative life force within you.

Tried and tested mantras are recommended, but seek expert advice before plunging yourself into an unfamiliar practice. Although the sound and vibrations of certain words can affect and awaken spiritual energies within us, it is advisable to seek professional advice from a qualified and recommended practitioner before trying more complex mantras or chants, as you may awaken certain energies within yourselves before you are ready to handle them. It is for this reason that we have concentrated mainly on easy-to-use affirmations, instead of giving readers something that may not be suitable for their development. If you wish to know more about mantras and how to use them, you will find four practical introductory books listed in the Recommended Reading at the end of this book.

The power of prayer

There are two kinds of spoken prayer: the affirmative and the kind that asks God and spirit to perform a particular act. With affirmative prayer, we have to be careful that it does not lead to a glorification of our individual ego, as nothing could be further from the purpose of spiritual unfoldment and we need to be on our guard against this happening. What affirmative prayer aims to achieve is to bring about a recognition of the unlimited creative spirit within us and within all life around us and helps us awaken to that power and influence.

The other kind of prayer is often misunderstood and used with little result by many, who generally ask in a half-hearted and half-believing way for something to happen (usually to a power that is separate from themselves), while at the same time attaching themselves to the problem that confronts them, dwelling upon it and giving it more strength and power over them. Needless to say, this is not the ideal way to use prayer. Instead, look at prayer in these ways:

1. Before asking for the fulfilment of any worldly needs, we should first seek a wider perception of life, otherwise we may find that what we are praying for is of little help to our spiritual growth. We must first have practical knowledge of the nature of God and spirit. If we have limited

ideas of our relationship to the spiritual laws that govern the universe, our practices will have limited results.

If we are to pray for anything, we need to first ask for more spiritual understanding, in order to become more aware and to realise that we are not separate from God or spirit – how we are all interconnected in one complete whole and God's power works through everything.

2. There needs to be conviction in what we are doing. Why bother praying if we do not believe our prayers can have an effect? So cultivate a positive approach to prayer, have confidence that it works and is a means by which you can empower your spiritual potential.

3. Leave things in the hands of God and spirit to do their work. Recognize there is nothing that God and spirit cannot do. This does not mean we should deny or suppress any problems that confront us. Only by facing life and understanding what is going on beneath our surface consciousness can we make progress in our spiritual unfoldment. Any emotional wounds we may be holding on to will need to be healed through a process of acknowledging that they are there, embracing and letting them in, giving them some space, feeling into and understanding what they are about and accepting them. Only then can the final process of letting go and no longer identifying with them really begin.

4. Prayer has to be used to stimulate and enhance our development and bring us to that point of recognizing that we too are spirit; that we too are part of God and give ourselves to this power in order to allow it to manifest itself more purely in us, through us and as us. We do not deny the physical dimension of life, but instead affirm that it is Spirit in essence: the body exists because of its Divine nature functioning through it and giving it life.

5. Strengthen your link with God and the spirit every day by making prayer a regular part of your unfoldment. Do not wait until trouble strikes before you decide to do this.

How prayer functions
The quality of our prayer will depend on our level of understanding and

our ability to be in tune with the spiritual dimensions of life. The power of prayer is found in the way we say the words, whether mentally or verbally. If there is true feeling and compassion behind our words, along with an attained level of awareness, our prayers will stimulate deeper levels of our being. The spirit in us, which is linked to the one Spirit in all life, will recognize and respond to the meaning of our words and will bring about corresponding results, using whatever channels are available to it. This is, in essence, what occurs in some forms of distant healing. Yet prayers and affirmations are not ends in themselves. They need to lead us to a state of receptivity where we focus our attention upon God and the spirit and strengthen our awareness of our spiritual being.

*   *   *

A personal realisation exercise

Be quiet and compose your thoughts. Make your link with the spirit, and find peace and strength in that contact. Affirm your relationship to the spirit world. Affirm your relationship to the Divine reality that exists in all life and repeat the following affirmation:

I recognize the supreme Spirit within me and acknowledge my oneness with all life. All is in harmony with my life. I allow the creative power of the spirit to flow freely in me, through me, as me.

Finish by disidentifying from anything that creates the appearance of separation from this creative power and by affirming that all these things are now done. (*Disidentification* is a term used by various contemporary teachers, which refers to the ability of being able to observe different parts of our psychological and physical selves, to acknowledge them as parts of us and also realise we are much more than them.)

Directing Thought

Teach me how to co-operate with your guidance,
and become rich in wisdom and understanding.

*I*t is said that God is Spirit and that we are also spirit, the same substance that is God. Various teachings inform us about living, moving and having our being in a spirit filled cosmos. But what can we do if we have not arrived at this level of awareness, whether in prayer or meditation, and discovered this truth for ourselves?

Initially, we need to consider the use of prayer and realise that it is simply thought rightly directed. 'Directed where?' you may ask. If we go back to the first statement that 'God is Spirit' and that we are also spirit here and now and possess within us some spark of the God-Spirit, it then follows that for prayer to be effective we must direct it first within and commune with our own spirit Self and overcome any appearance of being separate from it.

One way to proceed towards this is to sense this aspect of ourselves whilst using words aloud, such as, 'I know that God is within me as my own spirit, my own consciousness, eternity and creativity'. But what is more important than the method you use is that your unfoldment leads you to building a conscious relationship with God and the spirit and opens you to the creative principle within yourself. This can be achieved by using affirmative words, constructive thoughts and cultivating sensitivity that bring an awareness of God's and the spirit's presence.

Just as thoughts are living things, so too are our feelings and the words we use. This is why we need to be selective in what we think, feel and say in prayer, because of the creative principle behind all life and the law of cause and effect will come into operation.

First realise the God within. Talk to God as you would to a friend or someone you love. Let your prayer be natural and express just how you feel. Open yourself to God. As you do this you will find yourself opening up to yourself and the presence of spirit in all life. This is important as it will help you to be more self-aware and build a stronger bond between yourself and the Self that is both God and spirit.

Affirmations help you to keep your prayers alive and to be positive about yourself and your relationship to God. Understand the true meaning of what is meant by 'the presence of God'; that you, along with all life, have qualities of God within and that God holds nothing back.

Practising affirmative prayer

Make a definite time, twice a day if possible, to be alone. Sit down and compose your mind and think about God. Try to arrive at a deep sense of peace and calm, then assume an attitude of trust in that great power that is God. Next say to yourself the following:

The words I speak express the law of goodness and will bring about positive growth, because they are operating on the creative power of God that is within me. Good alone goes from me and good alone returns to me.

You are now ready to expand your positive affirmation. Begin by saying:

These words are for myself (speak your name). Everything I say is for me and about me. It is the truth about my real Self (think about your spiritual nature, the Divine reality of yourself – the God in you).

I know that God is the eternal source of goodness, light, love, wisdom and truth. These attributes are mine now at this moment because these things of God are within me and God's creative power is within me. The God within is the giver and sustainer of all life. I know that I (repeat your name) receive from this great power of original goodness all that I need for my spiritual journey. My every need is met now (state your needs).

I let go of all negative thoughts – I release them. I let go of all negative emotions – I release them. I let go of all doubts about myself and my pathway in life – I release them. I know that God and the spirit will guide and direct me to make the right decisions in life. I give thanks and so it is.

Statements such as this are not so much instructions to God, but are positive affirmations that remind us that God is limitless and is expressing itself as our individualised spirit and through us that self-same limitlessness. The more open we are to the Divine's influence, the more responsive we will be to gifts such as kindess, compassion, friendship and living in harmony with all. This operates through the universal law of cause and effect: 'as we think, so we become'. This statement can be seen as true in various areas of our lives. If we are little-minded, we receive little in return. If we are loving, we will attract love. If we are hateful, we shall attract hate. Laughter attracts more laughter. Joy attracts more joy and so on. So let us be realistic and honest with ourselves and remember that both God and spirit seek to encourage us to embrace the life we were born to live. Let us then be greater-minded and open-hearted that we may awaken to greater things.

Basic Steps

My life is one with my heart
and my heart is full of loving kindness.

A few decades ago the practice of meditation was looked upon as something mysterious and the people who practised it were considered somewhat strange. Today the overall view of meditation has changed. Most people realise that it can be done by anyone and that we do not have to be particularly religious in order to benefit from practising it. There is no danger in meditation provided that the practitioner is of sound mental health and sensible in going about the practice.

Many people have found meditation relaxing and of great help in today's stressful world. Certain types of meditation have proved to have remarkable results in calming the mind and relaxing the body. These are just some of the fruits to be discovered. Many teachers of meditation would agree that the ultimate aim of practising it is to bring about changes in our perceptions, as well as changes in our lives and interactions with other people and species.

Preparation before meditation practice
Meditation plays a vital role in the development of mediumistic, psychic and spiritual awareness. A sound and practical understanding of it gives us a strong base on which to build.

If you have never practised meditation before it is best to learn it in a meditation class or quietly at home. If at home, unplug the phone, close the windows and pull the curtains to avoid the distractions of exterior noises or sudden bursts of sunlight or car headlights. In time you will find these things will be less distracting.

Give yourself time to get into the right frame of mind. You may lead a busy life, but rushing into the practice and dashing off afterwards is an opportunity missed. Even if some benefit is gained, it will soon be lost. To slow down before or after a busy day, it helps to take some preliminary steps before you start:

1. Gather your thoughts before you meditate and bring to mind what you are about to do. Realise the importance of this time you have set aside. Put all exterior thoughts and concerns aside.

2. Because certain sounds and vibrations can make us more receptive to blending with the spiritual dimensions of our being, it can be beneficial to chant or listen to a soothing piece of music before meditating. Music can balance the creative and intellectual parts of the brain and enhance receptivity to intuition by bringing about a relaxed state.

You may at first find it helpful to use music during your meditation. As time goes on and you become more accustomed to meditating, it is best to limit the use of music purely to the preliminary stage of helping you relax and not during the meditation itself, as you might find your attention being drawn to the music instead of concentrating on your practice. Your mind might even start to conjure up images to fit the mood of the music. Nonetheless, it can be interesting to see how music affects you.

Extended vowel and consonant sounds can also be used and projected out loudly into the air, such as, 'O-o-o-o', 'A-r-r-r', 'E-e-e-e', 'O-h-h-h', 'A-y-y-y', 'E-m-m-m' or 'E-n-n-n'. These have a relaxing and focusing effect on the mind and body. If you try this exercise, exhale slowly and gently, projecting and concentrating on the sounds. Be aware of their vibration within the body and within the air as you sound them. Repeat each sound five times.

3. The place in which you sit can have a picture (possibly of a spiritual teacher you admire, a picture of a mandala or a scene from Nature) or some flowers that you find uplifting to look at beforehand. You might also wish to introduce an element of ritual into your practice by lighting a candle or some incense, arranging some flowers, or ringing a singing bowl or bell. All these can help draw your mind away from daily concerns and invoke awareness of the spirit within.

4. It can help to read a short passage or two from a book that inspires you, something that reminds you of what you are hoping to achieve in

your period of meditation.

5. You may wish to affirm your oneness with God and spirit, or send out a prayer which asks for guidance in your practice.

None of these are compulsory, but they may help you focus your mind upon the purpose of meditating and take your attention away from the events of the day and help you to concentrate better.

A place to meditate

Upon entering a place of worship you may have felt a strong silent presence surrounding you. This did not happen overnight, but developed over years through constant devotion and prayer, creating a conducive atmosphere for reflection upon God and the spirit. For this reason many prefer to set aside a room or place solely for the purpose of meditation. If this is not possible, then perhaps a special meditation cushion and mat or chair can be used, something that will not be used for any other purpose or be associated with any other activity.

Posture

Wear loose-fitting clothing or loosen any tight clothing, as this will help you relax and breathe better. If you sit in a chair, make sure it is comfortable, preferably with a firm back and not one in which you will fall asleep. If you can sit without support for your back, then sit more towards the front part of the chair. A small cushion under the feet can help raise the knees and straighten the spine. If you prefer to sit on the floor, the use of either a meditation stool or one, two or three firm cushions is recommended to bring your hips higher than your knees. This will help you to keep the spine erect and stop your legs from becoming numb. There are many different meditation cushions available, suitable for various sitting postures. Never sit completely back on them. A padded mat on which to rest the knees, feet and legs is also recommended.

Once in your chosen sitting position, gently sway your body slightly from side to side and from front to back. Try to find your centre of balance. With practise you should be able to judge this. If you are unsure, place your hands, palms up, underneath your posterior and become aware of the lower part of your pelvis pressing against your hands. When you move too far forward, it will feel sharp and when you move too far back, it will disappear. When you feel the pelvis pressing against your two hands without feeling too sharp, you should have found your centre of balance, though it should be noted that people who are thin in build may find the above suggestion painful and will find the pelvis sharp in their hands no matter what position they are in. The important aspect to remember is to keep the spine erect.

You may wish to use a cushion on your lap to rest your hands on to stop your arms pulling on your shoulders, or cushions under the knees, if sitting cross-legged, to give you more support and avoid strain on the knees. At this stage it is up to you how you position your hands. Many prefer to leave them palms up, resting on their legs, near to the body, either cupped one over the other or separate from one another. There are various different hand mudras that can be used in meditation that are said to bring about different states of awareness in meditation practice.

Your head should be at a level where your gaze naturally falls to the floor, approximately one metre in front of you. Let your jaw drop slightly, but keep the lips touching. This will help relax the facial muscles. Smile, then relax the smile, as this also helps relax the facial muscles. Keep your teeth slightly apart, with the tip of the tongue touching the front upper palate, just behind the front teeth. This helps to stop the flow of saliva and the need to swallow.

Try not to let your body slouch. Aim to keep your head balanced and your spine erect and make sure that you feel comfortable. You will be in the same position for a while and you do not want your body to start aching and distracting your attention. Some people find it helpful to imagine there is an invisible piece of string attached to the crown of their head that is being pulled up, which helps them to straighten their head, neck and spine. Keeping the spine erect distributes the weight of the body evenly and reduces discomfort during meditation practice. It also helps to keep you more attentive and allows energy to flow more freely through the body. You may find it difficult at first because your back muscles are weak, but with practice they will become stronger. Any slight trembling felt in the back muscles should disappear as the body becomes accustomed to sitting upright during meditation practice. If you find a part of the body starting to ache, it may be that your posture is not correct. Stop and adjust your sitting position and start again. If discomfort continues, it is advisable to seek expert advice about the way you sit.

Breathing and relaxing

It is beneficial to calm the mind and body before meditating and to check that you are breathing properly. The following exercises are useful for identifying and releasing any tension in the body and identifying any shallowness in breathing. More relaxation exercises can be found elsewhere in this book.

1. Lie on your back (or sit in your preferred meditation position) with your eyes closed and become aware of your breathing. Breathe naturally for a few minutes, then mentally check for any tension in your body and begin to release it without strain or force. Start with your toes and feet, then gradually work your way up to your head. Check that your fists are not clenched, your shoulders not hunched, etc. As you focus on each part, mentally say to yourself, 'My . . . (name the part) is free from tension and totally relaxed'. Be aware of your breathing as you do this. With each out-breath feel that you are releasing any tension.

If you have been lying on the floor, do not lean forward to get up as this can create tension in the neck and spine. Roll over on to your right side (or left if you find it more comfortable) and place your left hand (right hand if on your left side) on the floor, approximately one foot away from your chest. Then push yourself up by applying pressure to the floor with your hand.

2. This exercise can be practised in your preferred meditation position or lying on the floor. If lying on the floor, lie flat on your back, with your legs bent (knees drawn upwards), with your arms along the side of your body and the palms of the hands facing upwards. Concentrate upon your breath. Keep your breathing even. Check that you are filling the whole of your lungs with air. Your abdomen should rise and fall and your chest expand and contract. You should be able to feel this happening. If it is difficult to detect, it may be that your breathing is shallow and that you are using only a part of your lungs. Be aware of this and try to fill your lungs without straining or rushing – breathe a full, natural breath without force.

If you place one hand four fingers' breadth below your navel, you should be able to feel your abdomen rise and fall with each breath. You may be able to see your rib cage expand and contract. When you breathe in, try not to hold any tension in your body. Keep your abdomen relaxed. Let it slowly rise with the in-breath and sink down with the out-breath. It can be helpful to visualise the in-breath gently rising in a pyramid shape from your abdomen to your chest, or a 'V' shape from your navel into your chest area (use whichever you find most helpful).

If you are unsure about your breathing, you may wish to seek advice from an experienced yoga practitioner. Most spiritual centres will have someone who can advise you on proper and safe breathing practices for meditation purposes. But if in doubt about any advice you have been given, consult your doctor, particularly if you have health problems.

3. In your preferred sitting position, become aware of your breathing. Exhale gently through your nostrils and gently breathe in through them to the count of three. Hold your breath, without strain, to the count of three, then gently breathe out slowly to the count of three, emptying your lungs of air in a natural way without force, drawing in gently on the lower abdominal muscles at the end of each exhalation. Do this exercise five times. With each inhalation, breathe in all that is good and positive. With each exhalation, breathe out all that is negative. When you can comfortably breathe in and out and retain your breath to the count of three, increase it to the count of four, then five, but build up to this slowly over a period of weeks or months. This exercise energises the body and clears the mind, bringing both into a more conducive state for meditation practice.

If you have difficulty in holding your breath, practise without any breath retention until you are able to hold your breath comfortably without strain. Stop the practice if any discomfort is felt. We would like to warn against any drastic or prolonged changes to breathing unless under the direction of a knowledgeable meditation teacher, who can give guidance and explain the reasons for altering your breathing pattern. See also the following chapter on health problems and breath retention. As you do the above exercise, notice how your breathing changes your awareness. During the day, be aware of how your breathing affects you and how it changes depending on your state of mind. When you are calm, your breathing will be slow and even. When you are agitated, breathing becomes fast and shallow. Through breath awareness we can calm the mind. This is why breath awareness is so important in the practice of meditation. If you are attentive to your breathing, you will discover an important and integral aid to spiritual awareness.

*　　*　　*

A personal realisation

My mind is immersed in the spiritual dimensions of life. My actions are in line with spiritual living. I am an individual expression of God. I am whole and complete. My life is rich in love and goodness and open to infinite possibilities.

Meditation

Infinite Spirit, grant us your wisdom,
so that we may grow in true knowledge
and understanding of your ways.

*T*here are various methods and practices of meditation. Some involve breath awareness, visualisation or the repetition of a word or phrase. It is up to you to find a suitable practice. It is best to start with something simple and not to chop and change too often. However, you may need to try several types of practice before you find one that is right for you. Remember that if meditation is a new activity in your life, it may take time to master and understand. Be prepared to give it a trial period of at least three months.

Problems with health

Any healthy-minded person should have no problem with meditation. However, anyone diagnosed as psychotic or who is extremely neurotic, would be best advised to seek professional help first, as meditation practice may cause withdrawal into a world of fantasy.

If you suffer from high blood pressure, a heart condition, severe asthma or any respiratory problems it is best to seek advice from both your doctor and an experienced meditation tutor before practising, especially before doing any exercise that may involve retention of the breath. Certain yogic breathing exercises have been found to be beneficial in these conditions, but it is essential to check first.

If any breathing practices cause you problems, meditation can still be practised as long as your mind and body are relaxed, your breathing is rhythmic and your mind is focused upon the exercise. If you suffer from nerves, find that sudden sounds affect you or have a heart condition, do make extra sure that you will not be interrupted. Safeguard against any disturbance in your meditation period.

Meditation experiences

If you experience something out of the ordinary, do not be frightened as you may just be feeling something you are simply not used to. If it keeps happening and you are not sure that what you are experiencing is correct, consult a reputable and recommended meditation tutor before continuing. Many people experience such sensations as expanding or floating. This is natural and may be due to the mind, body and emotions adapting themselves to a new activity. Sensations such as tingling on the face could be due to becoming more aware of the skin's surface. They show how little aware we usually are of our bodily sensations. Do not try to repeat any of these experiences. Instead allow your meditation practice to progress and be a receptive and active process. Try not to become attached to any experiences or presuppose anything will happen. Instead trust your practice and allow it to peel away the outer layers of your personality and reveal the authentic spiritual Self within.

Meditation in action

When you are practising, let your breathing find its own natural rhythm (even if you are using a breathing exercise). This should bring about steadiness. Fix your mind upon your meditation. Let go of all concern for the outside world. Do not try to force yourself to concentrate. If your mind wanders, simply acknowledge this and bring your attention back to your practice.

Meditation is not about making the mind empty, which is impossible to do. Nor should it be a process of numbing your consciousness, but of strengthening and developing awareness of your mental processes in order to focus your attention and quieten your mind. At first, you might find it difficult to hold your attention upon what you are doing for more than a few minutes. But gradually with practice you will find that you will be able to focus your awareness for a longer period.

In the preliminary stages all kinds of thoughts may start rising to the surface. This happens because you have stopped to look at what is going on inside yourself. An analogy is often drawn, comparing the mind to a pond that has been stirred up. We often stir up our minds by feeding in all kinds of thoughts and emotions, but with the help of meditation practice we have the opportunity to transform troublesome areas, settle our minds and become more peaceful. Through this we are able to still the surface of our minds, look more deeply into our nature and discover our authentic Self.

Observing the mind in meditation and everyday life

When practising meditation you may find that your mind seems to become more active rather than restful. Old anxieties and experiences may start to surface. Emotions can rise up, the body may become fidgety and noises might distract you.

Observe these if they occur, but do not become involved in them or try pushing them away. Simply watch what is happening. One way to loosen the grip of such distractions is to identify and name them as they occur, i.e. 'body sensation', 'hearing sensation', 'feeling sensation', 'mind sensation'. But if a strong emotion does arise whilst meditating, you may need to look at it and discover what it is about before being able to disidentify from it. Meditation gives you the opportunity to do this. In some cases counselling may be helpful.

Observing the mind is a practice that can be done in everyday life. The following is a personal experience of a friend:

I remember waiting outside a railway station when an unstable individual tried to cause trouble just when some friends had turned up to be taken to see an Indian holy man I knew. I instantly saw several options, such as being justly annoyed, retaliating or playing the whole situation down so that it did not spoil my friends' evening out. I chose the latter and did my best to let it go. It was as though my mind had suddenly become like a multi CD player with a choice of which music to play.

The point about this incident is that there is an 'observer consciousness' behind the roles we play. This observer consciousness has the capacity to choose how situations affect us and how we react to them. By strengthening awareness of this ability to stand back, watch, observe and be attentive to what is going on in and around us, we become more knowledgeable of how we work psychologically and conscious of who we really are. As you go through your day, see if you can be aware of the choices you have in activities you undertake. Be aware of the many different roles you play in your daily life. See if you can be more aware of your observer consciousness. This is not often easy to do as we can get too caught up in our roles. Try to be aware that these roles are things you do and are not what you ultimately are.

Time and length of meditation

There is no set time or length to practise meditation. To begin with you may find 10 to 15 minutes sufficient. Many people prefer to practise early in the morning and at sunset, or before retiring at night. You may find it best not to practise too late as the mind may be too tired to concentrate. What is more important is the quality of your meditation, not its length or when you practise it. As you become more adept, you may find a longer period beneficial. A suitable length might be around 30 minutes, once or twice a day. If you have put aside a set time, there is less chance that it will be forgotten or missed because of other commitments. But even practising occasionally is better than not at all.

The reward of commitment

In the beginning you might be eager to practise meditation. It may be a new experience for you, bringing some instant benefit. But the mind soon becomes tired of routine and the pull of other interests and activities can weaken your commitment. This is when you will have to show some conviction in your practice of meditation and observe a degree of self-discipline. This may seem pointless to those who are restless and unprepared to make a proper commitment. But reward will await those who make the effort. Those who make even the smallest steps towards the discovery of their authentic Self will taste the joyful experience of finding deeper and more profound connections with life.

When you first begin to meditate you may on occasions feel that you are doing well and at other times that you are getting nowhere. Do not be quick to judge what you consider to be good or bad meditation. Continue with your practice. Do not think for a moment that any time you devote to mastering meditation is wasted. Remember that it cannot be measured by any experience, other than how it changes your perceptions of life and how you respond to it.

* * *

Breath awareness meditation

1. Sit in your preferred meditation position with your eyes closed, keeping your spine erect. Mentally check that your body is steady.

2. Bring your awareness to your breathing and observe the in- and out-breaths for one to two minutes.

3. As you breathe in, mentally say to yourself, 'I am breathing in'. As you breathe out, mentally say to yourself, 'I am breathing out'. Practise this for one to two minutes.

4. Keep your awareness on your breathing. As you breathe in, mentally say to yourself, 'I, a spirit, am breathing in'. As you breathe out, mentally say to yourself, 'I, a spirit, am breathing out'. Practise this for one to two minutes.

5. Let go of your awareness of your breathing for a minute and be still. Then return your awareness to the rhythm of your breathing. As you breathe in, mentally say to yourself, 'I breathe in spiritual energy'. As you breathe out, mentally say to yourself, 'I breathe out spiritual energy'. Practise this for one to two minutes.

6. Keep your awareness on your breathing. As you breathe in, mentally say to yourself, 'I am at one with God', and as you breathe out, 'I am at one with all beings'. Practise this for one to two minutes.

7. Let go of your awareness of your breathing and sit in the stillness, but continue breathing gently and naturally. Let the stillness and silence pervade your whole being.

8. When you feel ready, become aware of your body and your environment with a sense of well-being.

Being and Becoming

Make my mind tranquil and at peace
so I may reflect your love more purely.

*M*editation practice should become a natural and enjoyable part of our lives and its influence reflected in the ways we live. The following guidelines are given to help achieve success in this art.

1. Conduct and ethics

To obtain peace, balance and an inner and outer harmony, it is necessary to live decently and with a sense of order and simplicity. We must realise that we are all members of a global Earth community and need to honour humanitarian laws, as well as the laws of Nature and those connected with a spiritual way of life and living. This includes maintaining good relationships with our families, friends and working colleagues and finding meaning and purpose in our daily activities and interactions with other people and life. Through this we find ways of healthily contributing to life and discovering mutual beneficial enrichment with the natural world.

2. Living by spiritual laws

It is essential in our unfoldment to understand the implications of the law of cause and effect: as we think and act, so we become. We need to understand how this leads us to express the law of association and examine this law in our life – how we think, how our thoughts connect us with various levels of experience – and see if this is helping us awaken to our spiritual consciousness. Is this helping us to associate with God and Nature and realise that we are one with all life?

3. Synchronising our thoughts, feelings and actions

Our state of consciousness is the result of what we continually think, feel and do. If we wish to reflect finer qualities within us, we will need to gain some control over our thoughts, feelings and actions through practices such as meditation, inspirational reading, creative and selfless work and associating with people who are supportive and constructive in their outlook. All these will help us to move forward in our growth and help us to learn how to synchronise our thoughts, feelings and actions so they are in harmony with one another.

4. The process of spiritual attentiveness

In meditation practice it is necessary to collect together our scattered thoughts. We will need to be observant of distractions and learn how to bring our awareness to a one-pointed flow of attention, so that we change the flow of our thoughts from material matters and focus our consciousness within. One way of doing this is to bring your mind to a state of knowing the spark of the Divine within you, with the attention fixed at the point between your eyebrows. This is appropriate for 'thinking types'. For those who are 'feeling types', the attention can be fixed within the heart centre (middle of the chest) where the presence of the Divine can be felt. Just let your body relax. With your attention fixed at either of these two areas, you will find that your mental activity will gradually quieten down.

If you have difficulty thinking and feeling with attention, then start with breath awareness. You will soon feel yourself becoming calmer and more objective. Thoughts will still float into your mind, but you will find that you pay less attention to them and that they will settle down. Practise watching your breath until you feel you are ready to centre your attention on the heart or eyebrow centres.

5. Being attentive within

The more proficient you are at turning within, the more you will be able to focus your attention on meditation and the more positive and smooth your unfoldment will be. This will help you to become a more effective person, aid you to quicken your spiritual unfoldment and accomplish much more in life. You will find yourself more focused and decisive about the actions you need to make and becoming less out of sorts. You will learn how to live both inwardly and outwardly and success in these areas will follow. You will notice less failure and will start to become a person of purpose and insight, who knows no boundaries to spiritual living. You will then bring your spirit's true purpose into activity.

6. The secret of concentration

In all activities of life, particularly in meditation, we have to concentrate in order to perform any task well. When you sit quietly and become aware of the spirit within and as this awareness becomes stronger, realise that this inner spirit Self has its being in God – that God is within you and in all things, and how all things are ultimately in God. Centre your awareness upon this until it completely absorbs you. In time you may become aware of an inner light or a sense of joy and peace – an almost blissful feeling – or a greater sense of oneness with life. This will indicate that you are concentrating in the right manner. Whatever happens, give yourself to it, surrender your self to it, this is the secret.

To concentrate in this manner does not just mean thinking about it, or applying force to your thoughts. It is about letting your attention flow towards an awareness of the spirit within you and within all life – to let your conscious self merge and become one with the Divinity of all. In essence meditation is not yearning to receive, but allowing your attention to flow towards the Divine with a sense of aspiration. When you finish your meditation, you should always feel more at peace, happier and brighter. This will lead you to a state of oneness and joy in life.

7. A sense of oneness with all

As your meditation deepens, you will find Nature and life becoming more alive. Your life will take on new meaning. Your relationships with people and the world of Nature will acquire greater depth. Your ability to love will expand – you will find yourself becoming one with the Divine and will begin to realise that the spirit world is expressing itself through you and through everything and everyone. Try to remain conscious of this awareness throughout your day.

You will find that after your practice of meditation, your natural intuition will begin to function better, which will help and guide you in your unfoldment. You will find your consciousness becoming more open, aware and discerning.

*   *   *

A personal realisation

I live, move and have my being in the stillness of God. The light of the supreme Spirit shines through the whole of my being. My mind is quiet and receptive to the spirit within. I am tranquil, calm and at peace with all my thoughts and with all that surrounds me.

Stillness

I give myself to God so I may be used
in whatever way God chooses to express.

*T*here are four important areas of spiritual unfoldment: the use of words, the power of thought, contemplation and silence. These may overlap and affect different areas of our development. All can be used in different types of practice: in prayer, meditation, mediumship and in our daily life. They need to become parts of our natural life and through this empower our spiritual potential. But for any practices to be of value, we need to be on our guard against them becoming just dry routine and be conscious of what we are doing.

Transformation through contemplation

Contemplation is about introspection and reflection. It is sometimes called the 'Prayer of the quiet mind'. But in fact it is the stepping stone that leads towards that goal, whether in prayer or meditation. However, terminology can differ. Contemplative prayer in Christian traditions has comparisons with silent meditation practices in eastern traditions.

Contemplation helps us change our habitual flow of thinking from self-centredness to God-centredness. It focuses the conscious mind and develops our intuition so that our consciousness transcends worldly perception to more refined states of awareness. It helps us withdraw from restrictive patterns of thought and awaken to the Divine in all. Contemplation is the birth of spiritual attentiveness and is linked with the development of the quiet mind, as it is through contemplation that we learn how to slow down our thoughts and become more centred in God's presence.

If we look for the glory of God within ourselves and in the world that surrounds us, we cannot behold anything without recognizing its cause – the spiritual activity behind the outward appearance. As we stand in awe of this reality, we find fewer extraneous thoughts arising in our minds. The more we are able to do this, the more we will be able to realise God's presence.

Contemplative practice

It is initially through the analytical part of the mind that we start to open ourselves to God, by examining our thoughts and feelings and identifying anything that creates the appearance of separation from the world of the spirit. We can then overcome any barriers that we may have created around our hearts and minds and allow our intuitive nature to function and blend more freely with spiritual dimensions of life. Modern psychology has noticed two distinct functions of the brain. The left hemisphere is associated with analytical, logical, linear and intellectual thought, while the right hemisphere is linked to perceptual, organisational, creative and intuitive thinking.

In order to develop spiritually, we need to examine ourselves, our lives and our beliefs. We will need to find time to reflect and search our innermost selves. Remember you are the only person on this Earth who can truly know you, so discover who you are and how you feel about life. Face up to yourself and recognize the creative spiritual forces of life working through you. If you have the vision to see beyond the surface and look for the Divine's presence, you will discover a peace and oneness that pervades all.

Through the process of knowing ourselves we become aware of what is happening at deeper levels of our being. We become aware of what may need to be looked at, changed or overcome. We also discover all the potential good that is within us, find ways of bringing it to the surface and for it to have more influence on our lives and conduct.

Contemplation helps us to free our minds from past associations and to realise that there is more to life than just our bodies, minds and emotions. It helps us to connect more with all things. Take time to look for and experience God's presence within you and within the world around you. Look for it in the setting of a golden sun, in the sound of a running stream or in the rustling of leaves in the wind. Reflect upon all things and draw positive strength from them. Let all things awaken you to the God-spirit within. Let contemplation lift your consciousness in order to create an atmosphere of quiet receptivity where God and the spirit can be perceived.

It is at this point that contemplation overlaps into the next stage of awareness: silence.

The master key of silence

Silence, whether in meditation, prayer or mediumistic development is the most important ingredient for successful practice. It is in periods of silence that God and the spirit can influence us at deeper and more profound levels. It is here that our spiritual potential is often refined.

We should not be alarmed at the idea of silence, but let its mystery lead us to finding peace within – a peace that becomes the very heart of our spirituality, enriching our being and leading us to a deeper awareness of life. For it is not through intellectual reasoning that God and the spirit are found. They are reached through the intuitive mind penetrating and influencing our thoughts and feelings and awakening us to wider plateaus of being. This is not only accomplished through periods of quiet meditation, but is something that can be found in daily life activities and in our interactions with others through the development of an open and a receptive state of awareness.

You may wonder if what we are seeking is beyond intellectual understanding, does this imply that we are wasting the time we spend on books, vocal prayers or discussions concerning God and the spirit. It does not, because anything that can help us reach that point of attunement is of value. Time given to reflection, widening and focusing our consciousness will lead us to a personal awakening. All these activities can serve as springboards into the depths of direct experience. Until we have reached that stage, we will need as much help and encouragement as we can get and need such activities to replenish us on our spiritual journeys.

Stillness within

Let that inner stillness open you, so that you discover that sacred place within. Once achieved, you can rest, recollect and revitalise the whole of your being and awaken to the 'still small voice' that mystics of many traditions have found. In discovering this stillness, you will find that level whereby God and the spirit may influence and work through you and lead you to richer levels of being and consciousness. Do not be afraid of silence, but welcome it as a friend and companion on your spiritual journey. Share with it your whole self. Let it help you to help God and the spirit awaken within you the limitless potential which is yours. Let silence lead you to your higher consciousness. Let periods of silence, God and the spirit working through you, help you to understand the real you, as you really are.

* * *

A day working on yourself

Make time to be silent and quieten your mind, body and emotions. If at all possible, spend a whole day in total silence. Be aware of the peace and silence. Let it permeate your whole being and notice it in all things around you. Do not concern yourself with troubles of the outside world. Spend your day in prayer, reflection and meditation. Read a short passage from a spiritual book. Reflect upon the inner Self. Walk in the open air and reflect upon the one Spirit in all life. Let these activities encourage and help you to quieten your mind.

Sit quietly and ask yourself questions such as: 'Who am I?'; 'What direction is my life taking?'; 'Is there anything stopping me from unfolding my spiritual nature?'. See what this reveals and let it change your perceptions about yourself and your life.

Rest for a while in the spirit's presence. Select a word or short sentence that expresses your intention of opening yourself to the spirit. Say it once in your mind, then be silent and reflect upon it. If anything disturbs you in this time, repeat the word or sentence and go back to being still and silent again, but do not have expectations about what may or may not happen.

As you do this exercise, try to remain open and aware of anything that you may experience. If you feel moved to express your feelings by painting, writing or by sending out distant healing thoughts, then do so. Let the influence and inspiration of the inner Self come through into your daily life and activities.

You will find that days spent alone in silence will be of more value to you than you may realise. It is through such periods of inner silence and reflection that we strengthen our links with God and the spirit.

Exercises

Help me to embrace the physical, mental and emotional realms of being
and also to realise that I am much more than them.

*T*he following two meditations help to foster awareness and
sensitivity. They will help you to become conscious of how
your thoughts affect your unfoldment and will help to prepare your
conscious mind, so that any beneficial changes brought about through
these meditations become permanent fixtures within you. Once
established, every time you turn your conscious thought to these
meditations, your unconscious mind will know at once what is being
done and will help to bring about beneficial states for meditation
practice. This is why it is important to understand the role of thoughts
and feelings in unfoldment. It is why meditation is important, because
it changes our awareness. Without this change it would be difficult to
embrace spiritual realms of life and experience.

These meditations will help you to understand and work with the
spirit that you are and to lose all sense of separation from the Divine.
Through this you will develop a sense of openness to all possibilities and
start to awaken to the whole of creative life within and around you.

Awareness meditation 1[2]
This meditation helps to withdraw the conscious mind from outer
activity and focus it on your inner spirit nature. It will help you to
become aware of and affirm finer qualities. You may wish to use only
one or two of the qualities in step 5 and meditate on them for longer.

1. Sit in an upright but relaxed position. Let all tension go. Allow your
mind to become absorbed in your breathing. Watch your in- and out-
breath for about three minutes. Do not force the breath, but allow it to
flow evenly and naturally.

2. With each inhalation, feel your body and mind relax. Feel yourself to be alive and well. With each exhalation, imagine that all negatives, past and present, are leaving you. Practise for about three minutes.

3. Continue to concentrate on your breathing and mentally repeat, 'I am at peace'. Have a sense of being filled with peace, free from all tension and bondage. Repeat three times.

4. Pause for approximately one minute and breathe freely, feeling liberated from all restrictions.

5. Begin again, concentrating on your breathing and repeat the following phrases on the in- and out-breaths: in-breath, 'Love is my true nature'; out-breath, 'Not anger'. In-breath, 'Openness is my true nature'; out-breath, 'Not limitation'. In-breath, 'Acceptance is my true nature'; out-breath, 'Not denial'. In-breath, 'Compassion is my true nature'; out-breath, 'Not hatred'. In-breath, 'Freedom is my true nature'; out-breath, 'Not restriction'.

Repeat each pair of statements three times. After each pair, take a few minutes to absorb their deepest meaning.

Awareness meditation 2
1. Breathe in and feel within your breathing a sense of being at one with God. Repeat either of the following two affirmations:

God's power works through me, as me.

God's power, love and light fills my whole being.

Try to be aware of God's power within your whole being. Be positive and know that the affirmation you have chosen to be true. As you breathe out, be aware that you are one with God, that you are an instrument through whom God's power is pouring itself. Pray that God will help you to accomplish all that you need in your life. Stay with this practice for approximately ten minutes.

2. Breathe in and feel and know that you are one with God and the

spirit – one with your own spirit and the spirit world. As you breathe out, seek the spirit's aid to help you develop and to keep your life open to spiritual realms of growth. Do this for approximately five to ten minutes.

3. As you breathe in, breathe in a sense of God. As you breathe out, visualise your aura being filled with God's presence. Feel your aura expanding and connecting to a greater sense of oneness with the whole of life. Continue for approximately five minutes.

4. Finish by becoming aware of your body and the room in which you are sitting, then gently stretch. Take the experience of this meditation with you and allow it to influence you in your everyday activities.

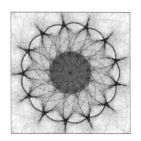

Part 2

Attunement

Proceed gently, sensibly and wisely.

Psychic Awareness

I behold the invisible in the visible.
I recognize its creativity manifesting through all.

People have understood and used psychic powers since ancient times. Their use can be found in nearly all religious traditions and indigenous cultures. The third section of Patanjali's *Yoga Sutra*, which dates back to around the second century CE, deals with the development of the *siddhis* (psychic and miraculous powers). Like the superknowledges in Buddhism, some of these powers are sought after in order to help yogis and yoginis overcome the effects of karma and attain spiritual freedom in their lives.[3]

Along with the *Yoga Sutra*, much has been written about psychic and mediumistic phenomena. Some writers believe that psychic and mediumistic abilities are detrimental to various areas of spiritual life. But this is only true if they are developed at the expense of spiritual awareness and practices of compassion, kindness, inclusiveness, unity, discernment and other attributes of a spiritual life and consciousness. Others believe that mediumship is a spiritual gift, separate from the psychic aspect of our nature. Some teachers of mediumship tell us that it is higher than psychic realms of knowledge – an altogether finer vibration that is separate from psychic abilities.

Yet if we look closely at mediumship, it becomes clear that it is a facet of our psychic being and is *not necessarily* a spiritual power if used in isolation from other areas of unfoldment. Like any other abilities we have, the responsibility of making mediumistic paths spiritual forces for good is down to us as individuals. In reality mediumship works through the same internal mechanisms of perception that we use to perceive regular physical life. For we would know nothing of the physical world if it were not for our psychic senses – every thing we perceive is processed through them. We experience everything in symbolic form, which has symbolic meaning to us, including language and all other sensory data.

We can know nothing of daily life until it is first perceived as a psychic image. So whether we like it or not, we are actually already living in a psychic world and the ability of mediumship also functions through it.

Yet on another level, *all life* – including the amazing workings of psychic activity in Nature and ourselves as interconnected parts of Nature – is a manifestation of God's goodness and creativity. This implies that psychic activity and powers, along with everything else, are facets of a spiritual source. In the end it is about the ways we categorise and separate things from one another that leads to differences of opinion. A holistic and an inclusive approach to and understanding of the whole of life and spirituality is the wisest path to follow.

Psychic and spiritual awareness

From one perspective, we see that the unfoldment of mediumship *by itself* does not require us to awaken to recognized qualities of spirituality. To become in tune with spiritual realms of life and action needs individual commitment and a deeper understanding of the Divinity of all. There are exceptions of course, where spirit intervention has happened in people's darkest hours of need, which has changed people's outlook and conduct. But this kind of experience may happen just once in someone's life, which means that being *open to* spiritual dimensions of living are our responsibility.

Mediumship is an ability much like any other. It operates through the mind. Its results are coloured to a certain or lesser extent by the character and personality of the individual. Some mediums have developed their mediumistic powers to a high degree, but have not displayed any change in their personal and spiritual nature. Another factor to bear in mind is that the majority of spirit communicators have only recently passed to the spirit world. This implies that they may not have spiritually progressed much more than when they were alive in the physical realm of existence. Therefore, having the ability to be mediumistically aware of them will not necessarily make us spiritual, any more than being aware of people in our physical world makes us spiritual.

The word 'psychic' is in fact a broad term that encompasses the spirit, our inner being, psychological nature and mind. Psychic abilities are about awareness of certain non-physical influences. People who have mediumistic experiences describe how they get an impression or flash of something, a sense of seeing or feeling someone. This occurs through the psyche and unconscious and conscious mind and connects with our individual nature and to the whole of who and what we are. Because of its connections with our individual nature, we need to ask ourselves if we are spiritually aware and are acknowledging spiritual precepts.

All these points are made not to discredit the views of others, but to emphasize that our spiritual growth is in our own hands. Even though any effort we are prepared to make spiritually will attract corresponding influences that will enhance our unfoldment, it is still up to us to take the first step.

Working at the level of our understanding

Sometimes we see mediumship working at a person's individual level of understanding. For instance, at a public demonstration a medium gave messages which, although accepted as reasonably good evidence by everyone he went to, were all to do with various material pleasures, such as a pint of beer, a bottle of Scotch, or a plate of prawn sandwiches! Some mediums give messages that are always centred around someone's clothing or jewellery, but give little evidence of a person's inner nature and character. This kind of evidence can be useful, but if mediums constantly work at this level and none other, it shows they have not taken a wide enough view of mediumship.

Levels of awareness

There is much that we still do not understand about the human mind and how to awaken to different realms of our spiritual nature. In the past we may have been influenced in our thinking by the beliefs of others. Now we must take the opportunity to discover for ourselves their truth or falsehood. There are problems in trying to distinguish too sharply between inspirational and intuitive knowledge, the psychic, the mediumistic and the spiritual, the prophet and the activist, the mystic and the seer, as there is no clear point where one of them ends and another begins. All have their origins in our being and are an expression of an interactive whole, which consists of our spirit, minds, feelings and bodies. All are but a flowing towards a discovery of the infinite potential in all.

These powers that manifest in our unfoldment are simply a means by which we can demonstrate that there is something beyond ordinary physical realms of experience. But ask yourself what it is: 'Psychic, mediumistic or spiritual?' Individual beliefs will differ about what these things may be and can cause conflict and confusion, whereas an all-embracing and inclusive outlook on unfoldment does not. So search and discover the truth for yourself – this is an essential facet of what spiritual growth is about.

A holistic embrace

If approached sensibly, psychic and mediumistic unfoldment can lead to understanding the whole of our being and bring us into harmony with all life. When development is interwoven with a dedication to awakening to our spiritual consciousness, it will lead us to an embodiment of its implications. Although our spiritual nature is already the ground of our individual being and is interconnected with the ground of all, we will still have to awaken to its influence. If we are to be representatives of the spirit – either as mediums or advocates for paths of spiritual living – our lives need be a reflection of the spirituality of all life. Psychic and mediumistic abilities by themselves are neither good nor bad; it is what we do with these powers and any insights we have into the spiritual source of all that determine their worth. If we learn how to use them wisely and selflessly and allow them to lead us to a greater understanding and way of being and healthily interacting with other people and life, they will become something of real value.

Psychic and mediumistic abilities are neither unnatural nor supernatural as they are a product of natural and intrinsic laws in all life. People who have had a premonition or followed up something as simple as a hunch, will have discovered how their psychic nature functions as an ordinary everyday facet of themselves. To deny these faculties exist can mean ignoring inherent and integral parts of our nature that are as vital as any of our five physical senses – we would hardly wish to stop any of those from working. Many have been born with psychic and mediumistic abilities. Many have found these abilities unfolding naturally through a variety of spiritual practices. Masters of yoga tell us that through practising yogic postures and breath awareness, psychic and clairvoyant abilities can unfold, even if we are not actively trying to develop them. The Buddha was well aware that practices of meditation led to possession of psychic and clairvoyant powers.

But whatever use these abilities may have, the purpose of developing them needs to be linked with an awareness of our true nature. They need to lead and open us to a wider vision of individual, social and global responsibility, which expresses itself in every area of our lives. This way the problem of any ability becoming a distraction to spiritual realms of growth will not arise.

*   *   *

Visualisation exercise
The following exercise is useful for developing your powers of concentration and visualisation and for stimulating your psychic senses from a visual and sensing point of view.

1. Ask a friend to sit quietly for you as a subject for this exercise. Visualise that you are together in a garden or meadow. Look about you to see what flowers there are. In the garden there are cultivated flowers of all types, whilst the meadow has a variety of wild flowers. Take time to observe the flowers. Get a sense and feel of them.

2. While keeping in mind the friend you are sitting with, allow your senses to be drawn to one type of flower that represents his or her character and personality. Describe the flower, its colour, its variety and say why it represents these to you psychically.

3. Now move on to another type of flower that you feel links with your friend's emotions and feelings. Say why this particular flower is indicative of these.

4. Let your awareness be drawn to another type of flower that relates to your friend's potential. Say why the image and colour of the flower gives you this information.

5. Now move on to another flower that draws your psychic senses towards it, one which relates to your friend's spiritual aspirations. Once

again, describe the information you pick up from this flower and to what the information relates.

6. Now move away from your friend and towards the spirit world that links with him or her. Become aware of a spirit presence that draws you towards another variety of flower. Ask yourself why this flower is being shown to you. How does it relate to that spirit presence? What message does it convey to your friend?

7. Blend with the spirit's presence and become aware of who he or she is and what this person is trying to convey to you. Ask why this personality is communicating.

8. When you feel that this communication is ceasing, sit quietly with your friend in the garden or meadow and start to perceive how Nature and colour speak to you.

Note: Those who are artistically inclined may wish to look for symbols and describe how they convey information to you. You might want to try this exercise by visualising yourself and a friend standing before an easel with a canvas and some paints. You then visualise painting shapes or a scene that depicts the main elements of the exercise and explain what they mean. Those who are musically inclined may wish to find musical scales, chords, songs or hymns that depict the main elements of the exercise. These visualisations are tools to give the mind something on which to concentrate and strengthen its powers of attention. In time you will let go of these props and allow the flow of the psychic self to function naturally.

The Aura

Widen my awareness, so I may grow
and receive more of your gracious light.

*T*he aura is constructed of many levels or different grades of vibrations. In literature about the aura and in accounts of those who claim to perceive it, we often find contradictions about what the aura is and of what it consists. It all comes down to investigation, perception and psychic awareness.

We are constantly learning more about the human personality. It may well be that there are levels beyond what we can perceive or understand, so any hard and fast approach to this subject would prove to be limiting. The following is a brief description and a personal view of some levels of our being, which relate to various levels found within the aura. By understanding these, we not only come to know and understand ourselves better, but also come to realise the various forces at work in all human life and how these connect us with different powers within Nature and the universe.

The spirit and interpretations of the soul and the causal body

The highest principle in all life is the spirit and it is this which gives life to physical form. It is the eternal 'I', the God within and links us with the creative principle in all life. It is the authentic Self, our original goodness, which seeks to encourage us to evolve and to provide us with limitless potential at various levels of our being. We therefore need to try in our unfoldment to understand this higher aspect of ourselves and observe how it functions through and can influence us. When we awaken to the spirit within as well as the one Spirit in all life, we open ourselves to a variety of possibilities and experience.

Some people believe there is a separate level for the soul, while others maintain that the soul is another term for the *God-spirit within*, what the Yogic tradition terms the *jivatman*. Some call this separate level the 'causal body', which is said to be the highest or innermost subtle body that veils the soul. The soul is also looked upon by some to be either the emotional psychological self or as the Spirit individualised – as the higher consciousness in human life and a vehicle through which the supreme Spirit expresses itself. Different writers and teachers tell us that it is through the soul that we come to realise the Divinity of all. Whether this separate level serves another purpose to intuition or is different from or the same as the God-spirit within, we leave readers to decide.

The intuitive and the inspirational

There is something in each of us which knows itself to be more than the body. We can term this state of knowing as being a high form of intuition. Its development can be likened to an echo of the spirit, something within our consciousness that keeps endeavouring to bring to the surface of our mind a higher sense of being. When this level is awakened to, we experience the Divine's creativity expressing itself in and through our world and universe. We discover unity in all life and through that unity inspiration flows as a creative force.

Intuition is an activity of the right side of the brain that draws mainly on unconscious material. It can function on a spiritual, mental or emotional level. Certain individuals experience intuition in the form of physical sensations, such as tingling of the skin or notice a tightening in the stomach – what some people call a 'gut feeling'. Intuition is often more developed in those who have a high degree of imagination, such as children and artists. Women are generally more intuitive than men, though the fact that just as many men as women can be artistic and the discovery of the 'feminine brain' in some men, shows that a *developed intuition* is not gender specific. It is of course an essential part of psychic and mediumistic awareness. On an everyday level, it functions in the form of hunches and feelings of knowing when one is on the right track.

The mental level: the will and the intellect

Both the will and intellect are important functions of the mind. The will is a product of the conscious mind and is something that can be used by it. Through the use of the will we can have control over conscious thought and behaviour and can therefore see how it is an important facet of spiritual growth. But the will cannot *directly* affect our unconscious instincts and behaviour, although it can have substantial indirect influence over them through conscious processes.[4]

The will is one of various mental activities that entails focusing our awareness in order to carry out specific tasks. This vital ingredient in spiritual unfoldment can be used to overcome inner conflict and negative character traits and be used to direct and focus our attention in periods of meditation.

The intellectual level is connected with activities of the left side of the brain, such as logical, rational and analytical thinking. Whilst our senses supply us with information, it is the intellect that tells us what it is we are sensing. There is some debate about 'Nature versus nurture', as to whether intelligence (a problem word for many to define and agree upon) is an innate product of the genes or if it can be acquired and cultivated. The truth must surely lie in a combination of the two.

Our intellect can be used for different types of thinking. On a simplistic level, we could perhaps talk of *practical* and *specialist* uses of the intellect. The first is about everyday life and understanding, whereas the latter is concerned with developed knowledge in a particular area. We might have specialist knowledge, but not be very effective on a practical everyday level.

It is important to balance the intellect with the intuitive level so that one does not inhibit the other. Although inspiration functions through the intuitive mind, our intellect can help to give it more form and structure. For instance, a writer may have a flash of inspiration and write wildly for hours. But after this period, the writer will often need to analyse the content, as well as edit and arrange it into more logical order and sentences. The ability to understand language and writing is also a left-brain activity.

Emotions: links with instincts and cultural conditioning

We all have natural instincts and emotions that work through our personality and character. It is through the mind and its connections with the senses that emotions are generated. Generally, we respond to sensory information by appraising things as potentially good or bad, after which feelings and emotions arise according to the judgements we have made. Rarely, if ever, do we experience one emotion on its own. Some take the extreme view that the emotion of aggression is something that we all possess instinctively and needs to be released. This can be done by channelling it into various activities, such as sport. Nonetheless, this does not fit with our experience of everyone we meet. A more accurate view seems to be that aggression can often be the result of environmental conditions and restraints. As humans we may feel impelled to socialise and have different types of relationships in order to fulfil certain goals, desires and needs. When we receive more than we expect, it often makes us happy. But when these needs are not met, it often causes frustration. This can surface in the form of aggression or in other moods, such as depression or apathy.

We also possess various automatic responses that we share with other creatures on Earth, such as the 'fight or flight' response, and we are not the only life form that displays affection. Cultural differences also have a large influence on the way we act. Different countries have different standards of behaviour that affect the way people emotionally express and conduct themselves.

On the whole, the emotional level of our being is about the way we act and respond to life and has much to do with the psychological and habitual self and our worldly personality and character. However, heightened emotions of love, awe and ecstasy can have a transcendent function. And as a product of Nature, a refined level of our instincts, like our higher Self, may be trying to encourage us to evolve and find our true place in a spiritual universe.

In development it is important to be aware of the various conscious and unconscious forces working within and around us – how they affect and influence our lives – and cultivate more positive qualities, such as compassion and openness. We also need to find ways of releasing any accumulated stress caused by modern living and be aware of basic needs for living a balanced and harmonious life. Through all these things we will evolve and discover more peace and a creative productiveness in unfoldment.

The physical level

Our bodies are made up of atoms that are the building blocks of all physical life. Nothing in Nature is wasted. Our physical bodies are the product of atoms that once made stars, plants and other life in the universe. It is within the physical body's aura that some mediums and psychics claim to be able to perceive disease and health problems (although some say that the latter are first detected in the energy body).

Linking closely with the physical level is what mediums often refer to as the 'etheric body'. Mediums tell us that every organ and cell has its own vibration and pattern of energy, which can be perceived within the auric field. Our bodies exist because of their spiritual counterpart. The spirit seeks to express itself through our bodies, minds and feelings in order to influence all that we do. A balanced combination of the spirit, the intuitive, mental, emotional and physical levels of our being will produce a balanced, well-rounded, holistic and integral approach to life and unfoldment.

The energy body

Surrounding and working within everyone there exists a non-physical level of energy and activity. It is affected by all other levels of our being, including our conscious and unconscious minds. Various mediums believe this energy is used in the production of mental and physical mediumship as well as in healing. Objective clairvoyants say that it can be seen surrounding the physical body. Those who are sensitive to it say it can be experienced constantly changing and working within and around the body. But what this energy is and what it does is by no means clear and has not yet been recognized by contemporary science.

There are various views about its function and use. Numerous people seem to perceive and interpret this field of energy in different ways and have varying ideas about the way it affects us as well as how we can affect it. The Chinese talk about '*chi* energy', whereas yogis and yoginis mention '*pranic* energy' and mediums teach about 'psychic energy'. Whether these are terms for what appear to be similar things or for different levels of activity is a matter for further investigation.

All facets interacting

All levels of our being will vibrate as a variety of colours within the auric field. These colours all have quite specific meanings connected to different levels of ourselves. Nonetheless, all levels are interconnected and influence one another. Some say that there are certain colours that are static. If this is so, we must ask ourselves why, as we are constantly changing, therefore, so must the colours within our aura. They may well represent potential that has not yet been realised. On the whole, the colours within the aura constantly alter as we change our thoughts, feelings, environment and so on. As we grow in our development, certain changes will happen within us that will be reflected within our aura. To understand what the various colours in the aura mean, we need to develop our intuitive, analytical and psychic senses and understand them in relation to the person with whom we perceive the colours.

*   *   *

Sensing the aura
The following exercises will increase your sensitivity to energies in the aura:

Exercise 1
To begin to sense the aura, place both hands together in an attitude of prayer. Draw the hands out to the level of your shoulders. Keep your eyes open and your awareness centred in the space between the palms. Slowly bring them nearer until you feel that you have an invisible balloon between your palms. This is the energy from your physical aura.

Exercise 2
Stand one pace back behind a friend, holding your hands up (palms facing forwards) and move slowly towards your friend until you can sense his or her aura, approximately two inches away from his or her shoulders. Try to sense the energy of your friend's aura in your hands. Ask your friend to recall different memories, such as those associated with joy and happiness, fear or hate, or thoughts of someone they love or loved who is either living on Earth or in the spirit world. Ask your friend to think of healing and to imagine various colours. See if you can sense a change in the energies around him or her and check with your friend the changes you felt.

Suggestions for further exercises
(a) If you are an objective clairvoyant, look at people and see if you can begin to perceive a sort of misty outline around them. Keep this in clairvoyant view and see what may build from this. If you see colour, be

aware that it emanates from the person. Try to understand what it tells you about him or her.

(b) Take a flower. Go beyond its physical shape with the mind and find out what you see and feel. Try to understand its energy.

(c) Hold an object that belongs to someone and use psychometry (the ability to feel an object psychically and pick up information relating to the person that it belongs) to sense the aura and see what information comes from it.

Psychometry is a useful tool as it relates to the aura and enables you to understand a person's psychic activity. It is one of the most useful abilities a medium can develop.

On another level psychometry can be used to link with the actual physical origin of an object, instead of people associated with it, such as information about the part of the world it came from, or what materials have made it.

Colour Awareness

The spirit within me houses original goodness.

To develop an understanding of the colours that can be perceived in the human aura, we need some knowledge of colour and how we view it physically, psychically and mediumistically.

Seeing colour

We perceive colour because of various wavelengths of light that are either absorbed or reflected by what we see. In 1802 an English physicist, Thomas Young, first put forward a theory suggesting that just as all colours in the spectrum can be produced by mixing paints of only three primary colours (red, blue and yellow), so too could our eyes contain receptors that are sensitive to these three colours, and that all other colours we perceive are produced from different combinations of just these three receptors. In 1964 this idea, known as 'Trichromacy Theory', was confirmed, but it was discovered that in humans the three receptors were in fact sensitive to red, green and purple.[5]

Every colour has its own wavelength. Red is said to be the longest. This then changes through the spectrum to violet, which is the shortest. Beyond this we move into ultra-violet rays and x-rays, which are beyond the normal human capacity of perception. Any coloured object we perceive absorbs all other colours in the spectrum, except the colour which the object is perceived to be. That colour is reflected by the object, which we perceive through our optic nerves. Our brain then deciphers the colour's specific wavelength and gives us the impression of the colour. Pure colours of light that are made up of a single wavelength are rarely seen by our eyes. For instance, the red of a flower, though consisting mostly of red, may have within it a certain amount of blue and green and will reflect these colours as well as the red. When all colours are absorbed by an object, it will appear black. When equal amounts of all colours in the spectrum are reflected, white light is produced.

When we see colours clairvoyantly, our brain, mind, instinctive and intuitive senses will perceive colour in very much the same manner as we do when seen through the physical senses. The mind deciphers colour by using the same process of recognizing colour wavelengths, as it does when seeing colours physically, except it does so without the normal everyday use of the physical eyes, because we are not perceiving physical colours. Yet the same principles of colour seem to apply to non-physical dimensions of life as they do to the physical dimension. If this were not so, we would not be able to classify correctly any colours that we perceive through our mediumistic and psychic senses.

The variety of colour

Whether we approach the subject of colour from an artistic, scientific or clairvoyant point of view, there are no strict rules when it comes to the theory of colour. We should realise that within just one single hue of colour, there is a tremendous range. For example, to the trained eye, it is possible to differentiate more than 50 varying shades of blue. If we then consider changing the tone of all these blues, by making them darker or lighter, we will discover within this single range of blue well over 100 colour variations. Adding yellow (which has approximately the same amount of variations) to the blue will produce an enormous variety of greens and bluish and yellowish greens. If we next consider using the colour red and also take into account the density or translucent quality of colour, the variations of all these colours will run to hundreds, if not thousands, of distinguishable hues and colour combinations.[6]

An artist's colour wheel

The spectrum is often divided into six or seven bands. The colour wheel on the top of page 73 shows various mixes of six colours found in the spectrum (indigo, the seventh band, falls in between the blue and violet area). In artist's terms, we can produce these colours by mixing pigments of just the three primary colours (red, blue and yellow) creating a complete range of secondary colours. Opposite each colour you will find its complementary colour (one which is made up of its exact opposite). For instance, on the opposite side to red you will find

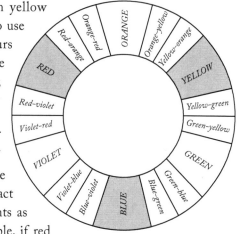

green, which is made from yellow and blue. If an artist were to use these complementary colours together, they would create the maximum visual impact; whereas colours closely related to each other on the wheel would create more of a sense of colour harmony.[7] But there is a difference between the way colours react and mix when using pigments as opposed to light. For example, if red and green paints were mixed together, they would create brown, but if red and green lights were overlapped, they would make yellow. The three primary colours are also different (see diagram below).

Coloured light

The diagram on the right shows spectrum colours formed by overlapping various proportions of primary coloured light: red, blue and green (called 'mixing by addition').[8] Mixed in varying proportions, these three colours can produce almost any colour in the spectrum.

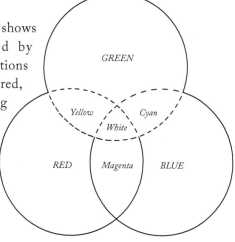

Mediumistic interpretation of colour

Though some colours may have an almost universal interpretation, we should realise that they can also mean different things to people and will affect them in various ways. Obviously colours have emotional meanings, but these may vary from one person to another. Also, a colour may change its meaning and interpretation when seen alongside other colours.

When we perceive colour in someone's aura, we should try to feel into the colour and link with that person without any preconceived ideas of what the colour may represent. We should look at the saturation of the colour, as well at its density or translucent quality. If you perceive colours clairvoyantly, you should remember the vast range of colours there are. If you see blue for example, ask yourself what shade you are perceiving. Are there hints of any other colours mixed with it? Is it a distinct, particular shade of blue? How dark or bright is it? What other colours are there around the colour? Only when you have done this should you seek to find out what the colour represents.

*   *   *

Developing an awareness of colour

The three simple awareness exercises that follow help to cultivate both an inner and outer awareness of colour. There is a danger of becoming too inward looking, so a balance between internal and external awareness is important. These exercises can put you more in touch with life both within and around you and help you to develop your sensitivity to colour. They are therefore helpful in personal, spiritual, psychic, mediumistic, social and environmental awareness.

Exercise 1: Inner awareness

1. Sit in a chair with your eyes closed and be still and quiet for a few moments.

2. Visualise yourself sitting in the middle of a room that is completely white. Imagine that everything in the room has been painted white: the floor, the ceiling, the windows and any furniture you see in the room.

3. Stay in this room for a few moments and ask yourself how it makes you feel. Do you feel cold, peaceful or uplifted? Or does this room make you feel agitated or indifferent? Whatever you feel, observe it and try to identify it.

4. Now try changing the colour of the room to another hue and see if you notice a difference in your feelings. Then try other colours and observe your responses.

5. Imagine that the room is completely green. Then visualise yourself in a forest, surrounded by different shades of green. Try to see these in your mind's eye. Feel into the colours and see how they affect you. See if you notice a difference between being in a green room and being in a green forest.

Exercise 2: Outer awareness
1. Find time to be alone in Nature and near some trees. Sit down or slowly walk around in a quiet and peaceful frame of mind.

2. Observe how much variety of colour there is in Nature. See how a single tree can have so many different shades of green in its leaves. If you do this exercise in autumn or winter, you will find a myriad of yellow-browns and reds in the colour of the leaves. Notice the play of light and shade on the trees and on the ground. Look at the texture and various colours in the bark of the trees. Observe the ground beneath your feet and how it is not just one shade. Notice how the colours in one tree are different from those in another and how different the colours of the trees are from any bushes or grass areas.

3. Now observe how you respond to the colours you are contemplating and see how they affect you. How do they make you feel?

This exercise can be done at any time and anywhere. As you walk down the street in a busy city you can observe the play of light and colour on the buildings and shops and be aware of how much colour and light there is in a street. Be open to life around you, conscious of how you react to it.

Exercise 3: Stretching your awareness and sensitivity
1. Collect a variety of different coloured plain (not patterned) scarfs, ribbons or papers. Place them in front of you and pick out one colour and see if you get a feeling or impression from it. Look at it and feel into it. Analyse your impressions.

2. Choose another colour or shade and see if you discover any difference.

3. Now place the two colours together and see if that tells you anything more.

4. Add a third colour and see if that changes your impression in any way.

5. Ask yourself questions about these colours and shades. Do they make you feel happy or sad, heavy or light? What kind of energy or vibration do you get from them?

6. Put the colours back and choose three, four or five to which you feel drawn. Tell yourself that these colours are to represent various aspects of your own personality and spiritual nature. See what you can discover about these colours and what they reveal about yourself. Make a note of what transpires during this experiment, as you may wish to refer back to it for direction later, to see how things have changed if you do the exercise another time.

This exercise can be taken a stage further by asking a friend and then someone you do not know so well, to choose some colours they are drawn to and see what impressions you get from them. Ask them to be honest and tell you how accurate you were.

Mediumistic Unfoldment

Help me to see with the spirit's vision,
to hear the sound of a voice long-still
and feel the closeness of those much loved again.

*M*ost mediumistic development groups sit in a circle. The reason for this is that it places the sitters equally apart and gives them their own psychic and spiritual space. The circle is a symbol of wholeness and unity. The initial motive of the circle and sitters should be to develop psychic energy and power over a period of time. This aids those in the spirit world to make their presence known.

If conditions are right, spirit personalities will bring their own energy and power to blend with the circle. It is through this blending that the sitters will in time come to know who is mediumistic. It will then become the responsibility of the other sitters to encourage the potential medium to develop trust and become responsive to the spirit world's influence. This is of course a very basic description of sitting in a development group. We do not wish to presume how the spirit world would wish your circle to unfold. This is part of the discovery of the sitters and we would not want to interfere with that on-going creative process.

Rigid rules and regulations, such as how or how not to run a development circle, and even minor matters concerning members sitting with their legs crossed or not, can be restrictive, not just from the sitters' point of view, but more importantly from the spirit's. Regarding postures, we ought to remember that mediumistic abilities can be traced back to early indigenous cultures that would have sat for their development in times before there were any chairs.

The following *guidelines* are given for you to reflect upon. Remember that there is no substitute for sound common sense and rational judgement.

Guidelines to consider for successful mediumistic unfoldment
1. Sitters
The sitters need to be sincere, well-balanced people whose minds are

open and hopefully of a spiritual temperament, whose main aim is to build a link of communication with the spirit world. The purpose of a development circle is for its members to progress to a point at which they open to the spirit's influence and through that discover various truths about the spirit. Crucially there needs to be an aspiration to move towards spiritual realms of perception.

2. Time and place

Sitting at a regular time and place is important because it brings discipline into your life and the development of the circle. As time goes on and somebody shows signs of mediumship, you will realise that this has helped to establish the right atmosphere and vibration. This will enable the circle to jointly assist in the unfoldment of various levels of mediumship.

3. Potential

Sitters may show signs of mediumistic potential. If you are unsure about your abilities, do not be deterred from sitting and exploring possibilities of potential.

4. Attitude

Respectfulness and the desire to be of use to the spirit world are essential, as is a willingness to dedicate time to explore and understand dimensions relating to the spirit world and its implications.

5. Co-operation

All sitters will need to learn how to co-operate with each other and the spirit world, as well as how to interpret any experiences they have whilst sitting. Keep a level head and do not attach ideas to anything that might happen, until it is proven beyond reasonable doubt.

6. Circle leader

One among you may be chosen to be the leader of the circle. This person need not be a medium, although you may know of an established medium who you can trust, who will be willing to act as a leader. The circle leader must be of sound mind, particularly as he or she will have a great influence on how the circle and sitters develop.

For the sake of the group and the spirit, the leader needs to possess compassion, honesty, fairness and sensitivity to people. If possible, the circle leader should also possess a basic all-inclusive grounding in spiritual matters and development.

7. Harmony and trust

Most important of all is that the sitters get on well, trust and encourage one another to grow in knowledge and understanding of the spirit.

8. Proceeding with development

In the beginning, sit once a week, for one hour only. Do not be tempted to sit for longer, unless directed by the circle leader or by the spirit, or unless all the sitters agree that a longer period would be useful. You will need to learn how to be still, receptive and open to possibilities of growth – meditation is particularly helpful in bringing this about.

You will need to be non-judgemental during your period of sitting. Only when the circle has finished and closed in prayer will it be appropriate to analyse constructively what took place during the circle, how each sitter felt and what may have occurred. But even here an open mind is required.

When you sit for development, your thoughts and prayers need to be focused on surrendering to the influence of the spirit, so that knowledge of their world may awaken within you. In the initial stages you need to develop a sense of stillness and silence so that you learn how to relax the body and quieten the mind. Your breathing should be natural, rhythmic and without strain. You will then notice that as your body and breathing harmonise, your thoughts will start to settle, your mind will become calm and a feeling of peace will pervade your being. This provides those in the spirit world with the right conditions to start the process of your unfoldment. At this stage you cannot do very much, except be receptive to all that happens.

Some suggestions for practical do's and don'ts

1. Do take note of any feelings, experiences or occurrences while sitting. For example, spinning, floating, facial or cobweb sensations, light bands around the head, bodily heaviness, changes in the rhythm of breathing, the desire to stand, the desire to speak, seeing pin-pricks or flashes of

light, or the feeling of presences – the impression of a person, male or female, tall or short, strong or frail, etc.

2. Do not interfere, but allow events to occur naturally. You do not know at this stage whether a sensation is due to a spirit personality, to the body relaxing, or to the effect of a change in your breathing pattern. Your aim simply needs to be about exploring possibilities and what might be happening.

3. Do enjoy, in a relaxed way, all that happens, even if it is just a feeling of being relaxed in the body and mind and a sense of well-being.

4. Do not be nervous about anything that happens. Nothing can or will harm you. Just continue to be calm, relaxed and at peace.

5. Do remember that the spirit are trying to make themselves known through your psychic and mediumistic senses. Understand that the spirit have to work through your mind and consciousness, so their task is difficult. Therefore accept that the circle may take time to develop.

6. Do not be quick to judge any experience as being genuine or imaginary, or any impression as being your guide or a specific person, until you are sure, beyond reasonable doubt, that it is so. This point is of great importance as psychic and mediumistic sensitivity can make people impressionable, so keep a level head at all times.

7. Do remember that you will go through some peculiar experiences. The more familiar you become with them, the greater your understanding, responsiveness and sensitivity will be. You will also expand the range of your unfoldment.

The circle's motive
The best advice for anyone starting a mediumistic development circle is to have plenty of patience. Be prepared to sit regularly over a period of time and let the presence of the spirit build. Do not try to force the circle's progress. This is why it is important to choose your group of sitters carefully in order to have no friction, physically, mentally or

emotionally. You need to have a common aim, interest and dedication.

An important aspect of successful circle work is the motive of the sitters. Ask yourself what your motive is behind your desire to sit and develop. It would not be advisable to sit if all you want to do is play around with psychic powers, as this is not enough for the spirit. Ultimately your motive needs to be about selfless service. If it is, you will find you will unfold greater gifts and qualities. The spirit seeks to help you discover your spiritual powers, which are and always have been inherent within you.

Go quietly about your work. Remember that your prevailing attitude of mind and approach will attract corresponding influences around you and in your development circle, so keep a check on your motives and your circle's reasons for sitting.

Understand the importance of what you are undertaking. Mediumship is about many things, not just phenomena. It is concerned with individual growth, developing a deeper sense of responsibility for all life and a greater commitment to truth and its dissemination. It is about realising the creative spiritual laws that govern all aspects of existence and seeking from the spirit the deepest knowledge of these laws and how to live by them. If we really want to do something worthwhile, it needs to have a higher purpose. No time spent in searching for spiritual understanding is ever wasted.

You will see from all these things that your efforts will enable you to unfold finer qualities in numerous areas. You can then lead by example. Through this, the all-pervading presence of God and spirit will work more freely through you in order to commune naturally with others and highlight spiritual spheres of existence.

*   *   *

A personal realisation

I am a pure and receptive instrument for the spirit. I am guided by a higher power that expresses itself in and through all that I do.

Mediumistic Powers

I realise that all is part of the Divine
and that the Divine is expressing its creativity through all.

*T*his chapter and the two that follow include various classifications of mental mediumship. We hope they will give some understanding of the many facets of mental mediumship, which can be listed under nine headings: (1) clairvoyance, (2) clairaudience, (3) clairsentience, (4) inspirational speaking, (5) inspirational writing, (6) inspirational drawing, (7) automatic writing, (8) automatic drawing and (9) varying stages of trance. It ought to be noted that certain types of spiritual healing can also come under the heading of mediumship, as they can require someone to act as an intermediate or medium between the person seeking healing and the spirit world.

Subjective clairvoyance

Clairvoyance manifests itself and functions in two ways: subjectively and objectively. In subjective clairvoyance the medium sees images and pictures that are impressed upon the mind. These are perceived by the medium as thoughts conveyed by a person in the spirit world.

Spirit personalities can project images and pictures not only of their features, build, manner of standing and so on, but also objects relating to when they were living in our physical world. Many subjective clairvoyants liken this way of seeing to looking at a photograph in the mind. They may also subjectively see and describe seeing written words, such as names and places. All this is perceived by the medium through his or her subjective consciousness. Yet our own minds and our ability to visualise play a role in enabling the spirit world to impress us through our unconscious mind, so that images can impinge themselves upon our conscious mind, which then create a sense of seeing.

Objective clairvoyance

Objective clairvoyance is a form of mediumship through which mediums objectively see spirit people, objects and other manifestations of a psychic and mediumistic nature by means of their psychic senses. It interlinks with physical processes of vision. Without this, the objective states of clairvoyance would not be possible. But although there may be the impression of seeing a spirit person visibly with the physical eyes, this is not so, because spirit communicators are not physical individuals. We see them with our psychic eyes.

Remember that the range and ability of both types of clairvoyance (subjective and objective) are governed by the rate of vibration in which they operate through us. Thus, one clairvoyant may see things that another does not because of the degree of difference in his or her abilities.

Some objective clairvoyants also possess what is termed as 'x-ray clairvoyance'. This is the ability to see objects through intervening physical matter. Clairvoyants with this ability can view the inner parts of the human body, diagnose disease and see the actual processes of healing and decay.

Trance clairvoyance

Trance clairvoyance occurs when a spirit personality becomes the actual clairvoyant transmitter and speaks through a medium. The spirit will influence the medium's consciousness and use the medium's physical mechanisms of speech in order to communicate information about him or herself or other spirit personalities that are conveying information to him or her. He or she may give a philosophical talk (popularly known as 'channeling' in New Age literature). The question of whether the medium is a subjective or an objective clairvoyant does not arise, as it is a discarnate spirit and not the medium that has taken over the proceedings.

Telepathic and other types of clairvoyance

Telepathic clairvoyance also has a subjective and an objective state and has to do with the clairvoyant seeing events happening to those still living.

There is also something termed 'travelling clairvoyance'. In this the medium may be aware of being present at and seeing events that happened in the past, or events occurring in the present or future. This type of clairvoyance can also be perceived in a subjective or an objective manner.

There is another type of clairvoyance that functions without the intervention of the spirit world. This is when information is perceived through the mind of the clairvoyant and through his or her own natural psychic and intuitive perception, in either a subjective or an objective way. Obviously people do not have to be mediums to have this ability.

Clairaudience

Clairaudience is the ability to hear spirit voices in either the subjective or objective states. Highly developed clairaudients will be able to identify voices as being male or female, young or old. They are able to describe them with all their inflections and accents. They can hear voices speaking in languages that are not their own and of which they may be unfamiliar, but will be able to convey the information to the recipient simply by repeating the words as they hear them. They often use phrases like 'They are telling me' or 'I hear them say', which indicates they are hearing clairaudiently.

In the case of hearing objectively, the sound of the spirit voice may be so real as to make the medium believe he or she is hearing audible physical words. But this is not so, because it is not a physical voice. The physical ears do not hear the information; it works through the psychic and mediumistic senses and is sometimes described by clairaudient mediums as 'hearing in the head'. One way to go about developing this faculty is to adopt an inner receptive attitude of listening and to remain expectant that you may hear something.

Clairsentience and clairolfactory

Some mediums have the ability of clairolfactory and are able to objectively smell perfumes or different odours connected in some way to a spirit communicator's life on Earth, such as the smell of hops if he or she worked in a brewery.

Clairsentience is the ability to sense and feel things about a spirit person. It functions on both the subjective and objective levels. We may describe impressions we receive through clairsentience as a feeling or sensing of a spirit person being of a certain height or build. We may feel and sense their character and personality, what type of work they did, what part of the country they lived in, and what colour their eyes and hair were. This happens inwardly, as though we intuitively know these things about the person.

In this state the medium could have a feeling of becoming that person in an almost physical way and exhibit the stance, mannerisms or other physical characteristics of the communicator. They might experience the sensation of loss of a limb and even adopt the person's mental attributes and characteristics. As these occurrences function through our psychic senses and have links with physical abilities of sensing and feeling, they are very much grounded in psychic realms of knowledge.

*   *   *

A personal realisation

I am in tune with the spirit universe. I am in harmony with all of God's creations. Divine intelligence runs through me, revitalising and awakening me to its dynamic presence.

Inspiration

*Free the spirit within me. Teach me how to know
and attain the way to unbounded and limitless potential.*

*I*nspiration of any kind is a spontaneous event and is a power that can transform and open our minds. Whether writing a book, composing a song or giving a talk, when inspiration comes, ideas will simply flow through our consciousness. Such acts of creativity link us deeply with the creativity of the universe, Nature, God and spirit. Therefore the value of inspiration in unfoldment must never be underestimated.

In mediumistic development we can often experience a sense of being impelled to speak spontaneously. Insights can flow through us from levels beyond our individual sense of self. But because thoughts and words are forms with which we are familiar, doubts may arise as to whether these are our own or come from another source. It is through the cultivation of an open awareness that we come to recognize inspiration flowing from other realms.

We ought to consider that in all aspects of mediumistic development, the spirit have to use the equipment we supply them. In the initial stages the spirit will have to learn how to penetrate our conscious and unconscious mind and influence the flow of our thoughts. They may have no means of vocalising their thoughts, so they will communicate by influencing parts of our mind. It is for this reason that we need both trust in and an open responsiveness to the spirit, as these supply the spirit with beneficial qualities to use. They will then be able to implement necessary steps required to prove to us that information is coming from them.

Inspirational speaking and drawing inspiration from all life

If at any time while sitting in a mediumistic development circle you feel inspired to speak, then do so. We suggest that you record or write down everything that is said, so that over a period of time you can look back and listen to or read what has been said and see if any changes have occurred in the manner of speech (if recorded) and the content and use of words.

However, it is important to remember that we can be inspired not only by individual spirit personalities, but also by events and experiences in our daily lives. Because we are spirit ourselves, inspiration can surface through our everyday awareness in a myriad of unique ways. This too is of course a highly valid form of communion with the inspiring diversity of life and can play as much of a part in our psychic and spiritual unfoldment as any form of mediumistic inspiration. Here again, a way to awaken to this is to simply be open and responsive to numerous things that can inspire us, such as Nature, music, art, beauty, poetry, literature, healthy interactions with others and the sacredness and Divinity of all, and how they can enrich our spiritual lives.

Inspirational writing

All that has been said about inspirational speaking applies to the impulse to write. Keep your mind open and receptive and avoid prejudgement of any writing as this can interfere with its flow. Whatever information comes, whether for yourself or another, look for evidence of who is communicating. Do not blindly accept things. If the information is philosophic, examine its content and be aware of the role your own mind can play in this form of development.

Some people may unfold the skill to write poetry. Again you need to reflect upon the source from which it is coming. Is it from your own mind, from an individual spirit personality, or from another unique source of inspiration? Look at the content and decide its value, no matter what type of inspiration has produced it.

Inspirational drawing

Some find themselves inspired to draw, even though they may lack artistic skills. Yet through spirit inspiration they find they are able to draw proficiently. At first the drawings may be crude in quality. But with patience and persistence they can develop into something exceptional, such as accurate renderings of faces of friends, relatives or helpers in the spirit world. You will need to look at the accuracy and the likeness of any drawings to the people depicted. Through this you will hopefully establish the reality of survival of those in the spirit world.

Some people develop the ability to draw the aura. They are often impressed or inspired to put certain colours on to paper. This may be for the purpose of analysing a person's character and potential, spiritually as well as materially.

With this type of development and with all other categories of mediumistic inspiration, it is wise to keep a level head and not make claims that it is coming from the spirit world or any particular spirit personality until you have acceptable evidence that proves this.

Automatic writing

With the development of automatic writing, some experience the sensation of minor electrical impulses going down their arm and feel as though their hand no longer belongs to them. People developing this ability might ask other members of the development circle for a pen to be placed in their hand, as they feel that someone wishes to write through them. If this ability persist, allow it to continue and observe the results. In the early stages, the writing can be just squiggles and swirls, almost childlike in style. Those who wish to know more about this subject will find further information in books by the automatic writing medium Geraldine Cummins, which show some possibilities and types of material that can be produced.

When writing, the arm and hand may move automatically. Through a process of suggestion we can withdraw control of our conscious awareness and allow a communicating spirit to take temporary hold over the workings of particular areas of the mind that affect various nerves, movements and muscles used for writing. Through this process automatic writing takes place. It will, however, depend upon the degree of which we can control the influence of our conscious awareness, which may affect any message and information given through this form of mediumship.

If our consciousness interferes, there will be a blending of our thoughts with those of the spirit. So here we need to consider two factors: the mind of the communicating spirit and the mind of the medium. A state of trance may be more desirable to eliminate any influence of the medium's thoughts. Yet even in the different states of trance, our unconscious mind can affect the message and its interpretation, which brings a third factor into consideration: unconscious control.

When automatic writing develops, experiments can be introduced to help remove any doubts about the validity of the material produced, such as blindfolding or placing the medium in a blacked-out room and then allowing him or her to proceed with writing when he or she feels ready. In the early stages, any material produced could be removed afterwards, so that the medium does not see it and so exclude any unconscious reproduction of work. You might need to proceed with such tests until the medium and the sitters are satisfied that it is discarnate information and is both reliable and consistent. Other tests in lighted conditions could then be introduced.

The medium and the sitters will always need to consider what level the information is coming from. Because our minds and the range of our thoughts are potentially so vast, it can be difficult to distinguish between inspiration connected with our own unfoldment and that of a discarnate spirit. In all aspects of mediumship, we need satisfactory evidence that it emanates from a source beyond our individual self and from a mind of a communicating spirit.

* * *

A personal realisation
I am open to receive and be inspired by the creative mind of the spirit.

Trance

Make me one with your eternal goodness.
Help me to serve with an open mind
and a compassionate heart.

*T*here are numerous degrees of trance, ranging from a state
of feeling inspired by a discarnate spirit personality to deep
unconsciousness. The latter brings about a temporary suspension of
ordinary awareness to external surroundings. In this state the medium
takes on and displays the character, personality and mannerisms of an
individual spirit communicator who wishes to convey information. This
occurs through the mind only – the spirit does not inhabit the body.
It is through the mind that the spirit influences the way the medium
moves and speaks and the content of what is said. In this state, the
spirit can even walk the medium around in a normal manner, with the
eyes shut or blindfolded. This demonstrates that a discarnate spirit does
not need to use the medium's physical sense of sight.

The influences of trance

Trance can be used as a means by which the spirit can influence and
awaken within the medium the ability to become a finer instrument
for teachings of spiritual wisdom. But we must not think that
merely witnessing this form of spirit education is the ultimate of
spiritual growth; it is only one of many ways that the spirit can
communicate with us. In its finest form, trance teachings aim to
encourage us to unfold our spiritual qualities and overcome limiting
patterns in our lives.

Trance, as in all forms of mediumship, is about co-operation. All
forms of mediumship need to heighten various levels of a medium's
perceptions, not just the psychic and mediumistic. If mediums allow
trance to affect them this way, the influence of a communicating spirit
will filter into their unconscious mind and affect and expand their
everyday conscious states of awareness.

Stages of trance

All spirit influence is actually a form of trance. All mediums, whether demonstrating normal clairvoyant, clairaudient or clairsentient mediumship, or speaking inspirationally, are in a state of entrancement. Even when mediums remain aware of all that is happening, a certain part of their mind will be influenced by a spirit personality in order to express information.

In the early stages of development we may feel sensations such as heaviness, cobweb-type feelings, tight bands across the head and body, tingling on the head and face and numerous other parts of the body, which *may* indicate spirit activity.

Types of entrancement

There are what are called varying 'light, overshadowing states' of trance where the medium experiences the desire to speak, yet feels that the words are coming from a source that is separate from him or her. What needs to be looked for in this type of mediumship is the quality of information and how it is expressed, i.e. whether or not there is a continuity of expression that would indicate the spirit's presence, such as philosophy that displays a high degree of knowledge, or concrete information that can be verified as unknown to the medium.

In the deeper states of overshadowing, mediums experience less control and selectivity of the information given through them. Though they may catch glimpses of what is being said, they are unable to perceive the exact words and contents; rather like hearing someone speaking in a distant room. This might indicate the potential of an even deeper state yet to be developed.

Development of trance

Because little is still known about the human mind and the multiple of ways people unfold their various abilities, it is difficult to be precise about how each potential trance medium should proceed with his or her development. This is where trust and spiritual aspiration play their part. Although the same power of the spirit operates through all, it manifests individually through our character, personality and mind.

The development of trance requires patience and the ability to be still, so that we enter into a state of silence, through which we withdraw our awareness from external activity to an inner state of consciousness. This needs to be accompanied by a responsiveness to all that happens during the time we sit. We will need to open ourselves to respond to whatever spirit influences register upon our conscious minds. This will quicken our psychic and mediumistic senses and will allow them to ebb and flow in ways that help us to become more aware of the spirit's presence. Through this the possibility for entrancement intensifies.

Because there are many factors that determine the rate of trance unfoldment, it is not possible to give any definite time in which this aspect of mediumship can be developed. The aim needs to be on meeting the spirit halfway and entering into reciprocal and conscious co-operation with them.

Circle sitters

We now come to the role that circle sitters play in the development of trance mediumship. Regularity and punctuality are essential. All sitters are required first of all to be level-headed and not inclined to jump to conclusions. They must be able to distinguish fact from fantasy and willing to devote their time and energy to the development of a potential trance medium. The sitters should not try to accomplish this by means of force, but by patience and accepting that the spirit may creatively draw upon energies they need to quicken the development of the medium in the direction they wish his or her unfoldment to go.

The sitters may observe certain changes occurring to the medium, which can indicate the development of entrancement. The medium may suddenly jerk slightly or experience vibratory, trembling sensations and report temporary loss of physical awareness. The medium might afterwards describe prickling on the skin's surface, like mild static shocks, or a feeling of wanting to stand and speak. Everything that happens should be accepted calmly and rationally, with no time limit, presupposition or restriction placed upon what is happening or when it will be developed. At all times the medium needs to be encouraged to carry on working until the stage comes when the spirit proves itself. When it does, the spirit may be asked for further direction and guidance for the circle.

With the unfoldment of trance, as with all mediumistic abilities, perseverance is essential. In the initial stages there is often very little to show for the efforts put in by individual members of the circle. Nonetheless, dedication will bring rewards.

Remember that this is an experiment by you and the spirit world and that both sides of life are endeavouring to co-operate. Therefore, you need not be discouraged by what may appear to be failure or by any long periods of inactivity, as you never know what your efforts have achieved and what changes you have brought about. Approach circle work as an act of dedication and selfless service to the spirit world and of creatively assisting in the unfoldment of spiritual wisdom and proof of survival after death.

Do not let discordant thoughts or disappointments affect the finer vibrations of the spirit, as these can have an adverse effect upon a medium's progress. It is for this reason that a harmony of thought and attitude in all aspects of unfoldment ought to be included as a part of the circle's development. Without it, successful development will be hard to achieve.

Trance in mental mediumship

In mental mediumship, trance may be used by an individual spirit personality to address us upon matters of spiritual wisdom and teachings. These can be of a general nature for a public meeting or of a more specific purpose for a particular person or a selective group. It might be used in a private sitting, enabling the spirit world to convey messages of more depth than *might* normally occur in other states of mediumship. Departed relatives belonging to a sitter may entrance a medium and give evidence of survival.

Trance can also be used in this form of mediumship for the public demonstration of trance speaking and *trance clairvoyance*, where the spirit *itself* conveys messages from *other* discarnate personalities. In general, trance in mental mediumship is confined to the small group, circle or private sitting. It is better for mediums to be guided by spirit helpers in the use of this aspect of mediumship, as they will know more about the development of and how best to demonstrate it.

Trance in physical mediumship

Trance in physical mediumship is used to enable the spirit world to work with energies necessary for the production of physical phenomena, such as direct voice where the spirit can be physically heard speaking, materialisations of spirit personalities and apports (the manifestation of physical objects). Yet we know little of what these energies are and what is entailed in their production. At times these energies may be visible, as in ectoplasm or small pin-pricks of light. They may also be experienced by the sitters in the form of sudden changes in the atmosphere or temperature of the room.

During entrancement the medium might experience sensations of discomfort in the region of the solar plexus or in the throat, or notice a general feeling of debility because some of his or her energies are being used during this state – similar to how energy is used in any activity but here in particular it is drawn upon by those working with the medium in the spirit world. The sitters too may notice physical pullings or gurgling sounds from these areas. These occur because spirit personalities are creatively using energies they need to carry out their work and to entrance the medium. Similar sensations may also be experienced in the unfoldment of trance in mental mediumship. It is for this reason that *all* circles members have something to eat and/or drink afterwards, to replenish any lost energy, though because physical mediums' heart rate and blood pressure often drop while sitting for physical phenomena they will need to wait until their body is back to a normal state before having anything other than water.

Physical and psychic energies used in this type of mediumship appear to be a combination of those from the medium and the sitters. These energies are then blended with energies from the spirit world and used to produce, vibrate and affect the atmosphere and environment of the development circle. Through this, spirit personalities can produce physical phenomena. However, the trance state is not always necessary for the production of these things.

Spiritual perspectives of trance and mediumistic unfoldment

We have already mentioned how the influence of trance unfoldment can enhance, encourage and stimulate spiritual growth. What needs to be considered is that after proof of survival after death, the message of the spirit is about personal and universal responsibility. Because of this, we need to develop from these trance states a more inclusive and globally responsible spirituality that cares about our Earth brothers and sisters.

Mediums themselves need to allow inspiring influences of the spirit to encourage them to become aware of, own and transform any negatives within their character and nurture more positive qualities that help them to face and overcome restrictive patterns of being and free themselves from the power of their expression.

Try at all times to cultivate a more expansive state of aspiration by means of prayer, quiet contemplation, meditation and drawing upon beneficial insights from the spiritual wisdom of all ages, as all these will aid and enhance further growth. At no time should you feel you stand apart from other people or regular activities of life, but instead integrate your experiences and knowledge with healthy everyday conduct.

Ultimately, as with all people following spiritual paths, mediums will need to consider how to unfold and develop a closer union with the Divine, with Nature and all of humankind. They will need to embrace ways in which to awaken within themselves a deeper creativity and appreciation of the awe inspiring evolving universe in which we live. This includes awakening to the Earth's natural beauty and to realms of love and wisdom, as this will cultivate mediums' minds and characters. This will widen and deepen the influence of their mediumistic potential and attract spirit helpers of wider knowledge. It will bring any potential medium closer to the spirit's sphere of influence and result in positive changes in his or her personality and spiritual growth. This in turn may prove the means by which mediums become greater influences for all that is good and an example through which humankind may be awakened to understand its eternal spirit nature more deeply.

*　　*　　*

A personal realisation
My life is the limitless life of the Spirit. My mind is full of harmonious peace. My heart is filled with loving kindness and full of purpose and meaning.

Physical Mediumship

Transform my consciousness so I will know of
no limitations and may awaken to greater things.

*T*his area of mediumistic development deals with how the spirit world can use physical and psychic energy and bring about materialisations of spirit personalities, dematerialise physical objects and rematerialise them again, or recreate the audible voice of a spirit through the use of a séance trumpet that amplifies the sound and/or a voice box made from ectoplasm.

Through this type of mediumship the spirit world can also build masks from ectoplasm for transfiguration and, by using psychic energy, move and levitate physical objects as well as the human body. They can create odours and perfumes seemingly out of nothing and cause raps to be heard (knocking sounds that can be used for basic communication). They are able to bring about changes in a room's temperature and create visible lights and luminosity. For those interested in knowing more about this type of mediumship, Leslie Flint's *Voices in the Dark* and Harry Boddington's *Materialisation* are highly recommended reading.

How to sit

For many years people sitting for the development of physical phenomena have sat in the dark. There is no reason why you should not do this and for any phenomena that occur to be genuine. But if you are going to invite strangers into your circle to witness phenomena that are developing, it is more advisable to sit under a good red light and so disperse any doubts people may have about their validity.

In some circles there is a small table in the centre and a cabinet curtained off in the room, in which the medium sits. However you decide to sit – whether seating someone in a curtained off cabinet or sitting with hands on the table to develop table-tilting phenomenon

– you need at all times to look to the spirit for guidance on how to proceed with the development of the circle, through whatever means they may wish to communicate with you.

Sitting for the potential physical medium

If someone is already showing obvious signs of physical mediumship, the lead may be taken from this, i.e. sit for that person to see what may develop. When it is not known whether anyone has such potential, it is best to sit in a normal manner with the intention that the spirit world will guide and eventually direct you to sit for one particular circle member.

The reason you will be asked to sit for this person is that all the energies – psychic, physical and mental – from you and the medium may be utilised for the development of physical mediumship. The spirit world will use these energies to experiment with the sensitivity of the medium and with the environment of the physical circle.

Progress in the circle

In the early days the proceedings may be erratic, irregular and rather clumsy. This is why patience and an open mind of everyone involved is essential. The sitters as well as the developing medium may have unusual experiences. It will take time for all, including the spirit world, to adjust to these changes. But whatever occurs, let it happen.

As development proceeds the phenomena may take on varying forms (as mentioned in the beginning of this chapter). But we should always be looking to the spirit for reasons why the phenomena occur and what value they have. The ultimate aim in this form of development is to prove survival after death and that there are powers both within and beyond us that can control physical activity.

During development, various trance states may intervene. This will introduce the circle and the medium to those in the spirit world that will work with them. You may eventually come to know the various roles they play in the different phenomena that unfold. Once the spirit have established their presence, they will be able to instruct the circle how best to proceed at different stages.

Be open to the spirit's directions. If you feel that its instructions are sensible and practical, then follow them and see if it helps the medium and the circle to move forward. Hopefully, events will go according to plan and the circle will make noticeable progress. But if little happens, go back to the spirit and seek an explanation, though do not accept anything that is given to you as fact until it is proven or has been assessed as sound, practical advice. The safest procedure is to question all that occurs and is said.

Those who develop these abilities will react to and develop them in individual ways because of their own psychic and spiritual nature and the spirit influences that work with them. There are no hard and fast ways of developing these powers. All members of the group need to proceed with caution and not allow any public demonstration of these abilities until all reasonable doubt about the circle's and medium's unfoldment and any phenomena produced has been removed.

We should not forget that because we are spirit ourselves, objects can be moved and all manner of physical phenomena occur through the use of mind-power, without the intervention of the spirit world. Parapsychologists and psychical researchers have noticed that in certain altered states of consciousness, ectoplasm can manifest without any definite form. But they have noticed that there is no evidence of a distinctly separate mind from that of the medium during these occurrences.

Realise that in all forms of mediumistic development that mediums are in a highly suggestible state and if we suggest things to them, they may take them on board unconsciously. This is why it is important never to form quick opinions about events that happen in your circle, but instead observe what is occurring without preconceived ideas. If you believe your circle is showing signs of spirit activity, it will be essential to prove beyond reasonable doubt that any phenomena are genuine.

*   *   *

A personal realisation
I commit my life to the one power that creates all.

Healing

Teach me how I may best serve you
and leave behind all thoughts of separation.

*T*he purpose of this chapter is not to condone or condemn any particular form of healing, but to encourage the reader to be open to its infinite possibilities. There are many forms of healing. Techniques include spirit healing, positive thought, prayer, absent healing and so on. Most methods appear to have their successes as well as failures. No one really knows why this happens. Some say it is to do with the patient's receptiveness to healing energies. An important factor is that the patient must want to get better. The effectiveness of healing may equally lie with the healer: with the ability to be an instrument for healing and allowing healing energies to work effectively and freely through him or her.

We should avoid laying the blame of non-healing at the door of the patient. The truth is that much of life is still a mystery. Just as we know that healing can relieve or cure, we also appreciate there are times when it does not. Healing in many cases is about acceptance of things as they are and making peace with ourselves and those around us, especially when it is nearing our time to leave our Earthly existence.

Self-healing and the transpersonal element
Techniques of self-healing are also varied. Many people are turning to affirmative thought, hatha yoga and visualisation and meditation techniques. All can be valuable in the process of returning individuals to wholeness and health, or helping them accept an illness with a positive attitude.

It is quite common for people to experience an instantaneous healing without the aid of a healer or any self-healing techniques. This often appears to happen in a person's darkest hour. Such a person, suffering from deep depression, perhaps near-suicide, may come to a point where they let go of all negative conditions, surrender and allow room for something else to take over. Such individuals usually experience a force that seems to be outside their usual spheres of awareness intervening and lifting their consciousness. They often feel united with an all-pervading reality that goes beyond ordinary physical realms of perception. A sense of timelessness is often experienced and all problems melt into insignificance. They may suddenly see the world as if for the first time and view all as being a part of one complete whole. They often feel and know that they too are part of all life. Some report seeing lights or spirit people, hearing voices or having out-of-body experiences.

An all-embracing feeling of unconditional love usually accompanies these experiences, which seems to touch the very centre of people's being. Yet it is the change that occurs within the individual which is significant. A transformation often happens alongside the experience. People's character and outlook upon life usually change for the better.

As some illnesses, whether mental or physical, can be an outward manifestation of inward trauma, such as stress, fear, worry, guilt and anxiety, we can clearly see why this change in consciousness is important in healing. Life may not become any easier for the people who have these experiences, but they may find the courage and conviction to face life with more understanding and acceptance. Many of the experiences described above are consciously unsought and come when least expected. But there are cases where people have deliberately visited a particular site to seek a cure and found it. Some have suddenly been restored to good health amidst the countryside or a natural scene of beauty. Animals also seem to have a healing effect on people. It is easy to understand why, as they can put us back in touch with life and remind us that we are all interconnected with Nature and the awe inspiring creativity of the Earth.

Some have even prayed to images of holy men or women and been healed. Yet none of these occurrences should be classed as unique to any single belief, as they all connect with the same universal law. It is only we who interpret this law differently and colour it with our ideas and beliefs.

The power that works through all
Various beliefs and theories have built up around the practice of healing. One would think that healing might unite everyone in the

common cause for good. Yet some practitioners claim the results of their work to be proof that only their way is right and condemn others because their beliefs, methods or views are different. Some maintain that others are working with wrong energies. This is not true, as the same power operates through all. We may, however, have distorted the use of that power by imposing restrictions on how it operates.

Whether we call this power that acts and creates in the universe 'spirit energy', 'the vital force' or 'cosmic intelligence', it emanates from the same source. It is the very essence of life itself, which permeates everything. It is the substance, continuity, activity and reality of all creation.

Confusion often arises in understanding this power when people expect it to work solely for those who view it as an expression or sign of their own beliefs. But this is not the way it operates. For it is indiscriminate – available to all. Some may try to place labels on it, but it will not make its use exclusive to anyone.

Whatever method of healing you use, let it be the means by which you discover this truth for yourself. Although healing is not accomplished by simply acquiring knowledge of the truth, it nonetheless helps us reach that goal and leads us to conscious union with the sublime power of God. As you turn within and relax in the realisation of your oneness with God, with spirit and with God as your individualised being, consciousness and identity, it will manifest outwardly as a demonstration of that unity. When you start to understand the many ways in which spirit energy functions, you will begin to shed old beliefs that have kept you from recognizing this. For it is both a learning and unlearning process that brings you closer to truth.

In touch with the purer self

The purpose of healing is to restore health, balance and harmony to those who are in need. Though the ways in which this can be brought about are many, the underlying principle is the same. Acknowledge that you are an individual expression of one reality (God) which works through you at your current level of understanding. As a deeper awareness of this reality is reached, it will manifest more fully. It will then work in and through you to a greater and less limited degree.

Your receptiveness to this power is your responsibility. If you are open to its influence, you will become a greater instrument for its demonstration. But be conscious that it is not through personal will-power that healing occurs, but through the unitive interaction of God and individualised being restoring any imbalance.

Because God's healing power has to function through our mind and consciousness, the more open minded and responsive to this power we are, the more free-flowing it will be in healing work. Let us not place any finite appearance at the door of the Infinite, because if we judge by appearances, we will become bound by appearances. Leave behind all beliefs that appear to limit this power and have trust in it. Just as when switching on a light you know it will release enough electricity to light up a room, so too, trust and know that the universal power of God will do its work. Even leave all thoughts and ideas of healing aside and become receptively aware of this power. This is what healers mean when they talk of 'getting themselves out of the way'. So do not concern yourself with appearances. Consider the fact that many people may go to a healer with the same physical symptoms, yet the cause of them might be very different.

If you are giving healing to someone for a particular problem, the last thing on your mind should be any thought that reinforces the appearance of separation from God and spirit. Be free from beliefs that tie you to person, place or thing. A healer once told us that he was short of time when giving healing to a group of people and forgot to ask one woman what her problem was. The next day she told him that a condition no doctor had been able to cure had completely gone. We see from this that although healers may have the desire to see a person well, they need not concern themselves with the illness, but instead remain unperturbed by any outward appearance. Another healer who achieved remarkable results with her healing work, always worked with the power of love and never with any thought of illness or disharmony.

Working with the power
Healers may be aware of energies working through them. Energy may be experienced leaving the solar plexus, or there may be feelings of something touching the crown of the head, of cold or heat emanating from the hands, or of uplifting thoughts. Some healers are said to have produced oil with a scented fragrance on their hands. People

being healed may also experience similar sensations of hot and cold, or a change in the body's energies, or feel vibrations, movements or breezes around the body. They may start to feel very relaxed and drift off into a sleep-like state through which healing energies may have greater effect. This can happen because they have let go of any worries or beliefs connected with any imbalance in the body and are allowing life-restoring healing energies to function more freely. In some cases the healer and patient may experience nothing at all. But this does not mean that healing has not taken place.

Healers may develop other gifts that can be used alongside their healing work, such as clairvoyance or clairsentience, and use them for diagnosis, or may even work in a light or deep trance state. They may be able to see or feel the aura and where there is a blockage of a patient's life force, as it is through the aura that healing energies are said to work. But more important than the methods through which healers work is the result.

Attunement with the universal life force

We should not take credit for any demonstration of healing. We do not use the power of healing, we merely let it work through us. Even to call ourselves 'healers' is misleading as we are not the repairers of damage or restorers of harmony – that is ultimately the function of the immanent and transcendent Spirit seeking harmonious expression through all.

Let us view healing ministry as a means of dedication and service and go about our work quietly and unselfishly, knowing that it is the power of the Divine, recognized and realised that does the work. Let us realise that this power permeates all and knows no limitations. It is the creative force in all life and seeks to express itself through us in the work we do. This does not mean we suppress or deny our problems. It is simply a matter of letting go and letting God and the spirit world take over.

We can attune ourselves to be more open to this power by various means of prayer, affirmation and meditation and by surrendering to a state of silent receptivity where we surrender ourselves to healing energies so that they may work more freely within and through us. A balanced outlook on life is essential, as well as devotion to spiritual living, for these will refine and enhance our unfoldment. Those of compassionate, caring and unselfish natures will obviously be more attuned to healing work. Remember that you are not just a centre of consciousness in but are an individualised expression of the creative power of God. Do not place any preconceived ideas upon what this power can or cannot do. Just let it be and let go of any ideas or concepts that create the appearance of separation from it.

*　　*　　*

Opening to the all-ness of creative unfoldment

The following is a lists of negatives and positives that create either the appearance of separation from the universal power of God and spirit, or awaken you to knowing your true relationship with it, so hindering or helping you in recognizing it in all things and all people – including yourself.

Negatives that create the appearance of separation from God and spirit	*Positives that help us become more aware and reflect our true relationship with God and spirit*
Anger and hatred	*Love and compassion*
Living other people's lives	*Living our own lives the best we can*
Prejudice and judging those who are different from us	*Unity and acceptance of the lives of others*
Selfishness and separation from others	*Selflessness and connecting with all life*
Superiority and indifference	*Giving oneself and being there for others*
Arrogant, irrational and uncontrolled behaviour	*Composure, balance and self-mastery*
Rigid and narrow views	*Openness of mind and thought*
Inflexibility and stagnation	*Flexibility and growth*
Spiritual pride and self-importance	*Self-awareness and humility*
Self-criticism	*Honouring ourselves*
Inferiority	*Realising our creative potential*

Delusion	*Seeing things as they are*
Ingratitude and receiving without thanks	*Thankfulness and awakening to the good we have*
Ill-will, greed and deviousness	*Goodwill, kindness and wholesome intentions*
Injustice and deception	*Fairness and truthfulness*
Confusion and doubt	*Clear and intuitive thinking*
Uncaring and mindless conduct	*Caring and mindful actions*
Disrespect	*Positive regard for all*
Impatience and hostility	*Tolerance and patience*
Agitation and conflict	*Peacefulness and contentment*
Thoughtlessness and vindictiveness	*Awareness and forgiveness*
Fear and anxiety	*Faith and trust*
Beliefs grounded in superstition and ignorance	*Beliefs grounded in truth and wisdom*
Depression and worry	*Wholeness and healing*
Suppressed and blocked emotions	*Open to life, joy and happiness*
Denying our feelings	*Letting in and accepting*
Holding on to negative appearances	*Letting go and letting God*

Exercises

I am one with all the creative power in the universe.

*T*hese visualisation techniques will aid you in developing deeper concentration and psychic and mediumistic powers. They can be safely practised alone or in a development group. These exercises will help develop awareness and sensitivity.

1. Either lie on the floor on your back, or sit keeping the spine erect. Close your eyes. Become aware of each part of your body in turn: the palms of your hands, backs of your hands, your fingers, feet, toes, ankles, calf muscles, knees, thighs, hamstrings, buttocks, back, shoulders, chest, arms, elbows, neck and head. Be aware of any tension. Wherever you find tension, let go of it as you exhale. Surrender it with your out-breath.

2. Turn your attention to your breathing. Find your normal rhythm of breathing, then visualise your whole body lying down or sitting (whatever position you are in) in the room that you are in. See your body completely relaxed and tranquil. As you are visualising this, become aware of feeling warm. Then imagine yourself becoming hot. Try to create this sensation and feel it as you would on a summer's day.

3. Now reverse the feeling. Try to feel cold, shivering cold, as you would on an icy day, in a bitter wind. Try to feel how chilled you would be. Feel this cold with conscious effort.

4. Next create the feeling of heaviness in your physical body. Imagine your body becoming heavier and heavier. Feel that you are unable to move any part of your body, even your eyelids. You are not even able to wiggle your toes or fingers because your body has become so heavy.

5. Reverse the feeling and experience the body becoming light. Feel the body becoming lighter and lighter until it is completely weightless. Imagine your body being so light that it is like a piece of cotton.

Do all this quite quickly with your thought. Do not take too long in trying. Just let the experience happen. Work on this practice until you can do it with concentration and intensity, as this will help you to be more sensitively aware of different feelings.

After you become proficient in this, you can visualise yourself holding different objects. For instance, see yourself (in your mind's eye) holding a piece of wood or cloth. Feel the texture of it within your hands, the length, the roughness or smoothness, the colour and so on. Imagine and feel the sensation of the chosen object. See yourself holding it. But use only your imagination and not the physical object.

You can also use colour or combinations of colour. Ask yourself how you feel about a certain colour and try to analyse your feelings. You can even visualise yourself talking to someone you know and to also see him or her talking to you. As the conversation develops in your mind, analyse the sensations you are experiencing. Try to feel what mood the conversation is in: joyful, peaceful, sad and so on. Then see yourself talking to someone you have met for the first time. Try to feel the mood of the conversation. Then visualise someone you do not like and notice any changes in your feelings.

Another exercise of this type is to visualise someone you have known who has passed to the spirit world. But in this instance, try to let your mind be open to what may come from them. As the experience occurs, listen to and see the person. In listening, capture and feel into what they are saying. As you look at them, ask yourself questions about them: 'Are they as you remember?' 'Are they younger or older?' 'Does there appear to be anything different about them?' Try to use your psychic and mediumistic abilities to become more aware of these impressions. Notice whether it is a genuine experience or just an impression conjured up by your imagination. See if you can distinguish a difference.

In practising these various techniques, you will be training your mind and senses to become more responsive. You will be refining your sensitivity to be aware of non-physical things so that when you seek communication of the spirit, you will be able to respond more strongly to their influence.

Practise each exercise stage-by-stage, but do not rush. Realise that it is you who is visualising. Do not accept any experience you have during the last exercise as being of a genuine mediumistic nature until you are absolutely sure and have evidence that it is so.

The purpose of visualisation exercises

Visualisation techniques are important as they can widen our creative and spiritual consciousness. They also provide the spirit world with more means through which they can work, as it is via the mind that they communicate. This is why artists can often make natural subjective clairvoyants because of their ability to visualise.

It is important to note that in conveying messages to and through us, the spirit can – and often will – use images that are strongly associated with things within our life and memory. For instance, you may regularly be given the impression of your mother or father as a symbol with which you can identify. It does not mean that the spirit world are necessarily saying that it is your mother or father communicating, but is a way of telling you that it is a parent of a person to whom you might be conveying information.

Visualisation exercise in attunement

An important stage in development is the link that we have with our spirit guides and helpers. The technique of visualisation we are going to describe is a means by which we can open our consciousness, so that contact and communication with spirit personalities may be possible. It should be practised with an open mind, with no preconceptions as to what may or may not come. Therefore it must be treated only as an experiment. The exercise is a creative visualisation in attunement. Even if you do not experience anything, it will help you to build your powers of attunement with the spirit.

1. Sit in a chair in an upright position (or in your preferred meditation position) and find your natural rhythm of breathing.

2. Consciously relax your body, then say a quiet prayer, seeking the aid

of the both God and the spirit to help you in this endeavour.

3. In your mind's eye, visualise yourself going to a location of your own choice, perhaps a favourite place that you know, a garden or somewhere you can easily visualise.

4. As you enter the place, find a seat to sit on. Feel relaxed, calm and happy about the possibility of meeting those in the spirit world who work with you. Be aware that you are going to meet someone or some people from the spirit world.

5. Keep relaxed and wait for the event to unfold. If it does not, do not worry as you can try again another time. But it is important at this point to keep the mind open and not conjure up images in your own mind.

6. While sitting in this place, be aware of what you are feeling. If someone appears to you, look at what is happening. For example, is the person talking to you or are you talking to them? Is the dialogue mind-to-mind or verbal? Check every detail of what happens, the reality of the experience and the impact it has upon you. Are you receiving any instructions or guidance? Observe and take note of everything concerning the experience.

7. As you approach the end of the exercise, ask whether this is a genuine experience or not. If you feel that it is, ask the person to prove to you that they are really there.

8. As the visualisation comes to an end, return with a feeling of joy, peace and serenity. Come back to yourself and sit quietly for a few moments so that the experience becomes grounded in your being. Acknowledge that you have taken a step in building your link with the spirit. Try each day to keep this awareness alive within you. Keep yourself open and receptive to unfoldment.

As you develop your contact and communication with the spirit world, you can develop visual mind journeys. For example, when communicators come to you, ask them where they lived and to take you there. Be aware of the locations and their homes. Let them show you the outside and the inside. Look for information that could be confirmed, like nameplates or numbers on the doors, or the names of streets. Learn to ask the spirit questions appertaining to their lives and their passing from our Earth. Seek their names and surnames and ask about them and others whom they have since met in the spirit world.

You need to learn how to probe with your mind so that you build between yourself and the spirit a dialogue of thought, vision, sound, feeling and sensing. Do not force anything or limit the capability of receiving information by having any preconceived notions or set views about what might happen. Have confidence in yourself.

Description exercises

In the demonstration of clairvoyance, clairaudience and clairsentience, the clarity of description plays an integral part. It is therefore important to develop the ability to interpret clearly and describe accurately what you see, hear or feel, as this will help to develop the quality of your mediumship.

Although the following mental exercises have nothing to do with psychic or mediumistic activity, they help in developing the ability to describe things more accurately. The exercises are designed to help you to use natural means of description to convey specific information. You will find that this will be of great value when it comes to conveying any mediumistic information.

Description exercises 1

1. Ask a friend to sit with you and then describe to him or her someone who is known to you both, but without saying his or her name. Try to describe this person's character, personality, sex, age, height, hair, build, manner, dress, distinguishing features, etc. See if your friend can recognize the person you are describing.

2. Describe details of a place, without naming the area, that is known to you and your friend. Outline its main features. For example, whether it is an area of a city or countryside. Describe any buildings, road layout and so on, and see if your friend can recognize the place.

3. Describe to your friend, without naming them, various types of objects in common everyday use, especially ones known to you both, which may be associated with people you know. Do not name the objects and see if your friend can identify them from your descriptions.

Description exercises 2
Listen to music of various types, or read poetry, descriptive novels or non-fiction, such as books on Nature, art or history. Notice how you feel as you read or listen and write down your feelings so that you remember them. This will help you to describe things that are more abstract, which is often needed in spirit communication.

Description exercises 3
Describe to a friend various emotions and feelings without saying what they are. Afterwards ask your friend to tell you what they thought you were describing and to point out where they felt you may have been unclear in your descriptions.

Psychic and mediumistic experiments
In each of the following three experiments, start by placing yourself in a calm and relaxed frame of mind. Try to be as descriptive as possible. Afterwards analyse all the information that came to you and determine how subjective or objective the information was.

Bear in mind that impressions or images of a symbolic nature may come, which you will have to probe in order to discover their true meaning. At first it may not be obvious that the impression or image is symbolic. The following observation by Santoshan illustrates this:

I once subjectively saw a monk, which at first seemed to represent a spirit communicator or guide. It was only after analysing this image and seeing how it looked more like a caricature than a real person that I realised it was a way of telling me that someone was connected with the surname of 'Monk'. On the same occasion I was shown lipstick being applied. This was a way of conveying the surname of 'Yardley'.

We see from these examples that it is necessary to probe any impressions or images and work with them, as our first and more obvious interpretations can sometimes be wrong. This is why it is important to ask questions like, 'Why am I being shown this?' and 'What does it mean?'. If you fail to do this, you may miss some important evidential information and what you give as mediumistic proof of survival after death will appear to be incorrect because you interpreted it wrongly.

Experiment 1

1. Ask a friend who you do not know so much about (perhaps someone who has only recently become a friend) to sit in a chair opposite you.

2. Put aside all that you know about your friend. Try to sense that friend physically. Find out information about his or her physical life without asking any questions. This could be related to your friend's character or work, or to the people with whom he or she works. Find out any information that could be used to prove that you are obtaining these details through your psychic senses.

Experiment 2

This is a basic exercise in which persistence will prove beneficial. Remember that mistakes are as helpful as accuracy.

1. In this experiment, try to obtain some information from the spirit world that links with your friend, which proves survival after death of the physical body. When seeking this communication, be aware if you are seeing clairvoyantly. If so, describe whether you are seeing subjectively or objectively.

2. Try to be aware of the communicator speaking to you. Notice how you are sensing. If you receive any information, pass it on to your friend. By doing this, you are bringing your friend into contact with all that is happening to you and encouraging him or her to be an active participant.

Note: As we have asked you to choose a friend in this experiment, it will be helpful to place all opinion and knowledge of him or her aside. You will find that doing this will help you to depend more on your psychic senses and the spirit world's influence.

Experiment 3

1. Ask a friend to bring some objects belonging to someone they know, without telling you to whom they belong. Take one of them and try to sense and feel to whom it belongs. Ask yourself whether the person is a man or woman. Attempt to find out about the character of the person.

2. Now seek to find out if the person is still living on Earth or not. If they are in the spirit world, try to gain some evidence that will prove they are actually communicating with you. If they are still on Earth, see if you can discover something that can be checked, such as the person's work or what he or she likes doing.

Note: Once you start to reach for some form of communication, we advise you to put the object down.

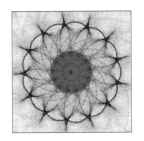

Part 3

Synthesis

Cultivate awareness, acceptance and letting go.

Self-awareness

Divine Spirit of infinite wisdom,
help me to find you in the depths of my being.
Show me how I may awaken to your omnipresent love.

*M*any psychologists believe the west is in spiritual crisis, that automation and rationalism have alienated many people from their true Selves, others and the natural world. Too much emphasis has been placed on external values instead of awakening to the unity we share with all life, finding inner peace, coming to terms with who and what we are and cultivating a proper balance between body, mind, feelings, spirit and Nature.

Through the unfoldment of internal awareness we can awaken to qualities of our true spirit Self, bring down any barriers that we may have created around our hearts and become more in tune with life around us. A part of this process involves becoming conscious of our basic needs, our individual nature and how life has moulded our current personalities and beliefs. With this comes the possibility of change and unfolding various potentials. We can each transform our overall selves and the direction of our lives.

Creative choice and growth

We learn about life from the moment we are born. Each of us sees life from our individual standpoint. What we have so far experienced, learned, felt, thought and achieved has shaped our psychological characters. Through trials and troubles we may have become more worldly individuals. But worldliness on its own may not necessarily lead us to discover a spiritual way of life and living and can lead us away from important growth.

You may have observed that the effects of any troublesome life experiences will not always help you deal appropriately with new situations, as we often let the outcome of such episodes influence us in negative ways. This can affect our judgement and cause us to react instead of being open and receptive to new experience. If we examine our perceptions of life we will find that they are invariable the product of past associations.

In the process of unfoldment we will need to break free from limiting patterns and seek to understand life from wider perspectives. If we cultivate an open heart and more positive qualities within us so that they interact with our feelings, thoughts and actions, we will be able to change our overall nature and live more skilfully. As you develop, you will notice negative feelings and thoughts caused by past associations beginning to loosen their hold. But this will only happen if you are prepared to let go of the past and be more receptive to and creatively interactive with the present. Only then can positive growth and inner healing take place and an openness to life begin.

The story of two travelling monks coming to a stream illustrates this. A woman asks if one of them would carry her to the other side: one of them does so. A while later, the other monk can no longer keep his thoughts to himself and says, 'What a nerve the woman had to ask monks to take her across the stream!' The other monk replies, 'Are you still carrying her? I left her by the bank of the stream.' The story shows, simply and profoundly, how we can hold on to experiences that bind us to the past. If instead we learn to live in the present and to be truly open to what is happening (interiorly and exteriorly), we will be able to use our experiences and knowledge of life in much freer and positive ways.

When we take up the challenge of knowing ourselves – physically, mentally, emotionally, psychically and spiritually – we discover ways of bringing peace into our lives and begin to view life from more compassionate perspectives. We grow in wisdom and understanding and learn how to bring all areas of our lives together into a unified whole. Through this we embrace the power of the present in wholesome ways.

Balancing psychic and mediumistic powers with spiritual paths

We often need time to transform any negative seeds and water the good ones for them to grow. If we seek to be in harmony with spiritual dimensions of life, we need to realise that the spirit knows no boundaries. Therefore we also need to awaken to a life that embraces all and overcome any sense of separation from other species and people.

We can become so entangled in the events of everyday life that we lose track of important spiritual insights. Unfortunately we have been educated to associate happiness with material things and believe the more occupied our minds are with self-centred activities, the fuller our lives will become. It is also wise to guard against developing psychic and mediumistic abilities with a similar outlook. For it is important not to become active to the point of developing and demonstrating these gifts only to find that we have little time to consider other types of growth and essential practices. There is a difference between *doing* and *being* and an even balance between the two is the wisest way forward.

Placing *too much* emphasis on the unfoldment and practice of psychic and mediumistic abilities can also lead to over-sensitivity, which then becomes a problem in daily life. If their cultivation is not integrated alongside such things as personal development and social responsibility, they will be of little help in the unfoldment of our complete personality and in discovering our inherent goodness, compassion and wisdom.

Overcoming the things that bind

Development ultimately involves including the whole. If we find areas of our lives in conflict with finer qualities of our being, it will be beneficial to consider ways for bringing about positive solutions, such as sharing our feelings and concerns, and putting ourselves in the shoes of others and listening to them. This involves both empathy and skilful flexibility and also accepting the infinite potential every one has.

Through being aware of deeper levels of our being we awaken to finer spiritual qualities. This is not about being self-righteous. It is about living creatively, obtaining a freedom of spirit that sees beyond the boundaries of limiting appearances. It is about self-growth, discovering the good within us and taking responsibility for our unfoldment. If we use a simple practice like breath awareness in everyday life, it will help to centre us and bring our attention back to our true spirit Self. By becoming more aware, we become more open, giving and compassionate, as awareness also encompasses being there for others.

When following spiritual paths we need to avoid activities that stop us caring about other people or life and allow the authentic spirit Self to guide us. Even if we sometimes fail, we should realise that growth is brought about in the trying, as we invariably learn more from mistakes than from achievements. It is also through acknowledging and accepting the negative parts of ourselves that we learn humility.

When we start to transform our lives, we may at first notice various negatives rising to the surface. We might discover aspects about ourselves that are not so pleasant. Do not be disturbed if this happens. Just accept what emerges and be positive about your growth. Noticing these things are invariably a sign of progression and signify that feelings that have long been denied are beginning to make themselves known. By becoming open, letting them in and owning them, you can start the healing process and start working towards letting them go and bringing everything into balance with your spiritual nature.

*   *   *

A personal realisation exercise

This exercise is a way of using the body to make you more aware of what is happening at deeper levels of your being.

1. Sit quietly with your eyes closed. Relax the body and mind and be still and quiet for a few minutes.

2. Become conscious of your body and breathing. Mentally explore the body. Slowly go through it and see if there is anything that draws your attention.

3. Turn your awareness to anything in your body that draws you to it. Feel into it and see what it is about. Ask yourself: 'Does it feel like tension or like a knot?'; 'Does it feel like a dull ache or a sharp pain?'; 'Is it something warm or cold?'; 'Is it a comfortable or uncomfortable feeling?'.

4. Do not rush. Wait and see what comes up and ask what it means to you: 'What is it about?', 'What is causing it?', 'What is it trying to tell me?' Do not rush. Feel into your body and be aware of what is going on.

5. Return to being aware of the room you are in and write down anything that surfaced during this exercise. This will help you to keep any impressions that you had and give you something to reflect and act upon later.

Individual Unfoldment

Guiding spirits, unite us in our understanding.
Help us realise that we are all expressions of the One,
that God is ever-blissful conscious existence.

*M*istakes are sometimes made by approaching development too narrowly. We must be wary of separating different areas of unfoldment into compartments and of having rigid ideas of how God and spirit affect and influence us, or of how we should develop.

To follow a set pattern to reach a specific goal with little concern for people's individual personality, character and deeper spiritual nature, is to assume that everyone is the same, including those in the spirit world. It shows that an open and wide view is not being taken. It is wise to investigate different areas of development in order to gain some practical knowledge, but this should lead to personal practice, experience and insight into numerous ways to God and spirit.

It is important to look at the whole, to realise that we are all different and that our environments, feelings, experiences, abilities, cultural and family backgrounds, beliefs, achievements, pains and pleasures will all affect our approach to development. It is from this viewpoint that we will need to consider spiritual and mediumistic growth and see what it entails.

Harmonising the complete personality

Since ancient times it has been recognized that there are various conscious and unconscious qualities or levels of the individual self: higher, lower and middle (positive, negative and moderate).[9] In order to bring about balance, we will have to look at what is going on at various levels of our being and find ways of harmonising opposing parts. Our consciousness is usually focused only around the middle area, with perhaps occasional glimpses of higher and lower aspects of our personality. Some try to deny or suppress the more negative, shadow parts of themselves. This can be dangerous as negativity will manifest itself in other ways. But even around the middle self, we are not always aware of what is going on.

If we become aware of our everyday activities, we will discover that we are many things: one minute the hard-nosed business person, next the loving parent and so on. Some of the roles we play in our daily lives may be major ones, others may not. Psychotherapists often refer to these different roles as 'subpersonalities'. We may slip into a variety of them numerous times a day. Yet it is through understanding all these levels of ourselves that we develop. It is through them all that our authentic spirit Self seeks to find harmonious and creative expression.

An instrument for the activity of the spirit

In the development of mediumship the same laws and power manifests through us all. We need to be conscious of how mediumistic gifts work through us and how they will be affected by our personality and character. Individual unfoldment is affected by how we and the spirit work upon the potential within us. It is also affected by our aspirations and willingness to co-operate with the spirit world and by the spirit's ability to influence us at various levels of our being.

Some people have tried to standardise methods of development. This has been partly due to them believing that because their method was right for them, it must be right for everyone. But because of our individuality, this is not so. We must never impose our ideas on others, or insist that others follow the exact pattern of development we have taken, as this can only be harmful psychologically and spiritually. It is God and the spirit working through our individuality, character and personality that needs be the ground on which our unfoldment begins.

Endeavour to link with God and the spirit influences that surround you and gain guidance and direction from them. Never allow yourself to be indoctrinated or to indoctrinate others. Instead, look at ways to encourage others and yourself to be open, straightforward, discerning and perform compassionate actions whenever you can. Through this, the influence of God and spirit will establish itself so that they and you will be of greater service to humanity and life on Earth.

* * *

A personal realisation exercise[10]

For the following exercise you will need a selection of coloured crayons and some sheets of white paper approximately 420 x 300 mm (18 x 15 inches).

1. Sit quietly for a few minutes with your eyes closed.

2. Ask yourself, 'What is it I want?' Fantasise about all the things you think you desire, a new car, a dishwasher, a house in the country, a new partner, a holiday in the Greek islands, a world cruise, a wardrobe full of new clothes, etc.

3. Next, make a note of them. Choose some coloured crayons you feel attracted to and free-draw any impressions, images or feelings that you get of them. Do not worry if you cannot draw. Those without an artistic eye sometimes display more freedom in their drawing, which can be equally revealing.

4. Put your drawing aside and sit quietly again. This time ask yourself, 'What is it I need?' This is a different question. Think about it and see what transpires.

5. Once again, make a note of anything that arises and draw any impressions, images or feelings.

6. Put the drawing aside and sit quietly. This time ask yourself, 'Is there anything that is stopping me from obtaining what I need?' See if anything comes to mind.

7. Make a note of what arises and draw any impressions, images or feelings.

8. Put the drawing aside and sit quietly. Now ask yourself, 'What is it that I need to do to overcome my barriers?'

9. Make a note and draw any impressions, images or feelings.

10. Place all four drawings and notes in front of you and assess your feelings about each question. Ask yourself, 'What do these drawings and notes reveal about me and my life?'

Transformations

Make my heart your loving home
and my life a true expression of the spirit.

*T*hrough knowing ourselves and opening to inclusive realms of spirituality, we balance our actions with creative living and become more centred and at one with all people and life. But a superficial interest in spiritual unfoldment will, however, not be enough to bring about this holistic embrace. We must to be willing to make some effort in order to awaken to richer, freer and more purposeful lives.

Be aware that everything you do, say or think will inevitably affect and colour your unfoldment. Every thought and feeling has the capacity to create either peace or discord, growth or restriction. If we consider the subject of absent healing, we see that by sending out compassionate and loving thoughts we are capable of bringing about positive changes. But if positive thoughts can result in healing, we need to consider the influence of negative and destructive thoughts, as they also have effects. Looking at ourselves in this way, we realise that we have responsibility for all that we do and think – a responsibility not only to ourselves, but to the whole of life around us.

Through self-awareness, we become more conscious of the positive and negative forces within us. We can then begin to become aware of ways in which to cultivate our more positive potential, transform our negatives and become more creative instruments for good.

Letting go and letting go into God [11]
Having some mastery over ourselves and learning how to let go are two important areas of unfoldment. Through self-mastery we strengthen our individual will, which should not be confused with a rigid self-centred will that makes us inflexible: "for there are higher things than the ego's will, and to these one must bow", Swiss psychiatrist Carl Jung reminded us.[12]

When our will is developed in a beneficial way, it helps empower our commitment to spiritual living. It also gives us the strength to let go and to disidentify from the appearance of any negativity. Through letting go we surrender ourselves to greater wisdom that intervenes and influences our lives and brings about positive growth. Surrendering includes recognizing that we cannot bring about a total change in our life and unfoldment without the aid of God and the spirit. Both the will and letting go are important in helping us work on many levels of our personality. It is through the will that we find strength and courage to face troublesome qualities, while letting go allows us to release them and to be freer and more open. Through creative use of the will and letting go we take responsibility for our lives and transform all that is of no value for the roads ahead. By doing so, we make room for the higher spiritual Self to influence and interact with our unfoldment.

Swimming with the tide

There are often many ways of approaching life. We can live it in a perfectly natural and accepting way, or rigidly impose different desires on how we wish things to be. The latter can of course achieve results, but it is like swimming against the tide and often leads to conflict and disappointment.

If we balance our lives with our authentic spiritual nature by cultivating wholesome awareness of our thoughts, feelings and actions and observing regular practice of prayer, contemplation and meditation, we will open ourselves, quieten our minds and see life as it is and experience it without limitations. For when we see things as they are we overcome boundaries and not only understand life and ourselves better, but also start to understand, feel and be impelled to do more for others, which is the true meaning of compassion.

Acceptance

Acceptance does not mean that we become inactive or passive. If properly used, acceptance becomes a creative tool, which naturally helps us in our unfoldment. It is an integral part of the growing process. Through it we learn to live skilfully and in harmony with all and take an active part in life. When we give ourselves to this life, we embrace God in all things and find that in return our lives are enriched by being embraced by God.

Handling experiences on the path

Travelling a spiritual path is not so much about seeking experiences, but unfolding our spiritual nature and allowing it have more influence. Nonetheless, important life changing experiences of various kinds can happen. They may occur slowly and gradually. There may be periods of sudden mystical, spiritual, psychic and profound mediumistic experiences (deeper to what we might normally experience), then nothing for months. At these times, things may be occurring at deeper levels than we are aware of. Periods of spiritual dryness, such as the Dark Night of the Soul, can happen. But by going through such episodes we often encounter new strength and insights.

As important and beneficial as some experiences can be, we ought to be careful of holding too tightly on to them, as this can block future progress. We also need to be watchful of believing a particular experience makes us more special than anyone else, but instead let the influence of any episodes open us and expand our awareness in positive ways.

Awakening to inner light

By awakening to spiritual dimensions of life, we have the capacity to become more centred and loving. In place of limitations we open ourselves to joy and freedom and embrace life in compassionate ways. Through healthy unfoldment we become aware of the spirit that we are and awaken to the Divinity of all.

Let the appearance of anything that separates you from recognizing this dissolve. The tangible living presence of God and the spirit will come easily to those who are pure and compassionate in their hearts and open in their thoughts.

* * *

A personal realisation

I am one with the infinite, loving Spirit. I release all discord and negativity from my life. I am an authentic representative of eternal goodness. I practise non-injury in thoughts, words and deeds and realise that all is equal in the eyes of the Divine. I am selfless in my actions, truthful and open to myself and others. I follow God's and the spirit's directions and perform all actions with the aim of growing closer to spiritual living.

Openness

Seeing into the nature of all things,
I awaken to a life of truth and openness.

*L*ife is about growth, starting from small beginnings and evolving into maturity. All life needs the right kind of nourishment in order to grow healthily. All around us, life can be seen in an infinite variety of manifestations, which is both creative and expressive. We should realise that we too are part of this life and just as everything in Nature requires food for growth, so do travellers on spiritual paths.

Nourishment can come from prayer, meditation and contemplation, or from lectures, reading and speaking to those with insights into spiritual unfoldment. Yet merely reading or listening to others speaking about spirituality will not by itself increase our spiritual awareness; for the spiritual life has to be lived. Knowledge can be invaluable, but life is the ultimate training ground. For knowledge to have creative use, it needs to be both practical and transformative and lead us to fuller expression and growth and a greater understanding of unfoldment. When it does, it helps us overcome all sense of separation from vast oceans of life around us and truly live an all-inclusive spirituality.

The universality of the spirit

If we study the lives of those who have travelled spiritual paths before us, we can be inspired by them and uncover practices they found helpful and various truths they discovered. If we allow their words to take root in our consciousness, their insights can motivate and help us to understand what living an authentic spiritual life entails. On the surface we may find contradictions to what we and others believe. But it should be remembered that everyone will see things from an individual position. The following story which can be found in many cultures about three blind men who try to describe an elephant illustrates this. The first blind man feels one of the elephant's ears and says, 'It is large and like a rug'. The second feels a leg and says, 'It is round and firm like a pillar'. The third feels the elephant's trunk and says, 'It is long and like a pipe'.[13] Their descriptions are not wrong, but they do not describe the complete reality.

Diverse as teachings of spirituality may seem, there are always many threads of common ground to be found. When we examine people's search for spiritual dimensions of life, we are looking at their quests to find eternal truths. In understanding the teachings of the world, we come to appreciate many cultures and various ways in which we can grow and realise our true nature. Too often we limit unfoldment. Concepts are often built around experiences. To believe that only one tradition or type of development has all the answers and discovered all there is to know about life, can only cause divisions instead of unity with our global brothers and sisters.

The one quest – with an infinite number of paths

If we are searching for greater wisdom to live by then we need to be receptive to growth and overcome restrictive ideas about life, spirit and ways in which we can develop. Those whose spiritual eyes are open will put differences aside and will see the supreme Spirit at work in all. Yet spirituality often challenges accepted standards of thinking and can sometimes trigger negative responses in those who are not ready to grasp wider truths. We are after all, creatures of habit and do not like our worlds being turned upside-down. Yet we should never force spiritual beliefs on anyone, but instead encourage ourselves and others who are searching to be more open and compassionate and make our lives the examples by which we are measured.

We always need to be moving towards wider possibilities of growth. It is not enough that knowledge is handed down from one to another. We still need to find, experience and learn for ourselves.

Spiritual evolution

To develop ourselves we have to be willing to progress and be open to new knowledge and experience. If we are set in our views, we are in danger of restricting the spirit of our own being. Through the cultivation of open minds and hearts, we connect more deeply with our true Selves and others, become in tune with all life and overcome inhibiting concepts that create barriers to spiritual living.

Realise that one reason for searching is that no one has *all* the answers. Let new knowledge and experience open you to fresher fields of vision. For if you wish to develop, what you may think of as important today may look different to you tomorrow. This is not to say that what you have so far discovered and believe to be true is false, any more than a view from a mountain's peak makes what is seen from the ground incorrect. In obtaining this wider outlook you will find all areas of your life evolving more naturally. By seeing beyond limitations, you will find truth in all things. Although your body is made from physical matter, its true essence is spirit. So allow your spirit to shine through.

Underlying the wondrous diversity of life there is one reality manifesting in an infinite variety of ways. Some call it 'God' or 'Spirit'. Others say it is beyond all words and concepts. To this reality you owe your very existence. In order to become a more receptive instrument through which it can express itself, you will need to engage creatively with life and embrace all the potential good within.

*   *   *

A personal realisation
I treat all people equally and embrace a life of freedom, truth and openness.

Exercises
Ideas for daily life

Lead me forever onwards to the spirit's understanding.

*T*he exercises in this chapter are simple practices that can be incorporated into your daily life. They are designed to help you become more conscious of your thoughts and feelings and more positively aware of your actions. One or two practices have been mentioned briefly elsewhere, but what we hope to do in this chapter is suggest ways in which you can implement them in your life. Unless you suffer from a particular health problem, you should not find difficulty with anything that follows. If you do, then ask yourself why. Is it because there is something that you are not facing and accepting within yourself? Remember that resistance can often be felt before a door is opened.

To the following exercises could be added others, such as chanting mantras or incorporating an element of ritual that connects with Nature in some way. You must discover what is best suited to your life and seek out practices that will be of benefit to you. You are in charge of your own development.

Having a regular programme can help establish a solid base from which you can draw strength and guidance in your life. Try to practise at a regular time. You will be less likely to miss your practices if you make them part of your daily routine. Give yourself plenty of time to do any of the following exercises. Do not rush them. Your attitude to the whole day starts here.

1. Upon awakening

As soon as you awaken, gather your thoughts and become aware of your entire body. Feel its weight upon the bed. Mentally become alive and visualise energy and life going into every part of your body, into every muscle, joint and cell. *Gently* tense and release your muscles and stretch your limbs. Become conscious of yourself, aware of the precious gift of life running through you. Arise slowly and consciously. Stand up and inhale fully through your nostrils whilst raising your arms forward to shoulder level. Hold your breath for three to five seconds, according to your lung capacity. Breathe out, lowering your arms to your sides, and let go of all tension. Sense peace and calm entering your body and mind. Allow them to permeate your room and environment, even if you live in a noisy city.

2. Prayer

Gather your thoughts, focus your mind upon the supreme Spirit and voice a simple prayer. Do not do this glibly; put feeling behind the words.

Example:
Gracious Spirit, guide me through the coming day and help me to establish your light and love within.

3. Preparing yourself

As you perform your morning ablutions, observe your actions and the sensation of water touching your body. Feel it bringing life and vitality to your skin and body. Water is a vital substance of life and is considered sacred in many spiritual traditions. Indeed it is, life cannot survive long on Earth without it.

Bathing is important, not only because it has a soothing effect on the body, but also because it soothes and refreshes the mind. It opens the pores and allows toxins to escape and so helps us to become more healthy. Sip a cup of hot, boiled water on an empty stomach every morning. But be careful doing this. The emphasis needs to be on *sipping small amounts very slowly*. This encourages good action of the digestive system and is a natural remedy for purifying internal organs.

As you prepare yourself for the coming day, be aware of your actions and thoughts. Whether you are brushing your teeth, preparing the children for school, getting dressed or combing your hair, do it mindfully and in a tranquil frame of mind.

4. Physical exercise

Because your body is the temple in which your spirit resides, it is a good idea to start the day with some form of physical exercise. This will help keep your body supple and free from tension and your mind more focused. Exercises are not just for the physical body, but also have a spiritual purpose. To help you be more aware of this, you can use affirmations with your practices, such as, 'I have strength and life in my whole being', 'I am centred in awareness', 'God's peace flows through me, in me, now'.

Some may wish to practise hatha yoga at this point, whilst others may prefer something less demanding. Simple exercises for loosening up the neck and shoulders will stop tension building up in these areas. Briskly patting the whole of the body, face, arms and legs with the palms of your hands has a marvellous energising effect. Whatever you decide, do it gently and rhythmically, putting life and energy into your body. But note that any form of strenuous physical exercise should be performed on an empty stomach. Wait for at least three hours after your last meal, and half an hour following a drink.

We would recommend that anyone who wishes to know more about yoga exercises should consult a qualified teacher and get expert tuition before practising on their own. Do not try to learn yoga from books or DVDs as you can easily strain or damage yourself if you practise wrongly.

5. A short reading

Spend a few moments each morning reading a short passage from a spiritually uplifting book. This will help bring the mind to a more responsive state for meditation later on and uplift and encourage you in your practice.

6. Relaxing and breathing exercise

Remember that breathing is the most vital force of energy. It is a form of nutrition, just as food is. The following relaxation and breathing exercise will help relax the mind and body and put you in a more conducive state for meditating.

1. Sit in a quiet place, where you will not be disturbed. Sit or kneel with your eyes closed in your preferred meditation position, keeping your spine erect.

2. Mentally check for any tension in your body, starting with your feet and slowly working your way up to the top of your head. Be aware of any tension being held in parts of your body, paying particular attention to your neck, shoulders and facial areas. As you go from one area to another, mentally say to yourself, 'My .. . (name the part) is free from tension and relaxed'. Release any tension with the out-breath. Once you have completed this exercise, mentally tell yourself, 'My whole body is now free from all tension and is totally relaxed'. This exercise should take approximately five to ten minutes to do each morning.

3. Bring your awareness to your breathing. Exhale through both nostrils, gently pulling in on the lower abdominal muscles at the end of the exhalation. Using your right hand, place your thumb at the side of your right nostril and stop the flow of air through the nostril. Do not use too much pressure. Gently breathe in through your left nostril to the count of three or five, whatever is most comfortable. Then gently breathe out through your left nostril to the count of three or five. Do this five times.

Place the third (ring) finger at the side of your left nostril and stop the flow of air through it. Gently breathe in through your right nostril to the count of three or five. Then gently breathe out through your right nostril to the count of three or five. Do this five times.

Keep your awareness on your breathing and gently inhale through both nostrils to the count of three or five. Then gently exhale through both nostrils to the count of three or five, carefully pulling in on the lower abdominal muscles at the end of each exhalation. Do this five times.

At the end of the practice, sit quietly for a moment and mentally say to yourself, 'Peace, love, harmony and goodness'.

If you do these exercises each morning, they will help keep your nasal passages clear and your mind refreshed and alert. Retention of the in-breath can be introduced to the last breathing exercise to the count of three or five, but only if it feels comfortable. Do not strain or force your breathing. Stop the practice if any discomfort is felt.

7. Using sound to evoke body awareness and focus the mind
Sit in your chosen meditation position with your spine erect. Close

your eyes and slowly inhale a deep breath. Then gently close your ears with your index fingers (do not apply too much pressure) and make a gentle humming sound as you exhale. Repeat three to five times. As you do this, be aware of the sound vibrating within your body and the air around you. This exercise can help relax and focus the mind before meditating and help energise the body and mind.

8. Meditation

This example of meditation can help to bring the whole of you into balance: body, mind, emotions and spirit. It should take approximately 20 to 30 minutes to practise each morning. It can be lengthened slightly by first envisaging a deeper shade of the following colours, then perceiving a lighter pastel shade.

Relax and breathe normally, slowly and rhythmically. Then breathe in the following colours. Do not rush from one colour to another, but spend time with each. Note the change in vibration of each. Feel it permeate the whole of your being.

1. Imagine and breathe in the colour red. See this colour as being quite bright and luminous and slowly sense it coming up from the Earth. Feel it entering into your body, balancing and spiritualising all organs, making every part of you function optimally, in harmony with itself. Feel it energising your entire being.

2. See this red change slowly into a vibrant shade of orange, coming up from the Earth and bringing vitality and health to your body.

3. Next, picture a bright yellow coming up. Feel a clearness of mind and a relaxing of your body.

4. See this shade of yellow change slowly into a rich, luminous green coming horizontally all around you. Within it, feel the natural vibration of Nature. Feel at one and in harmony with all life.

5. Now picture and inhale a bright luminous blue coming from above. Feel its calming, peaceful influence upon you. Know that this colour is restoring health and balance to your body, mind and emotions.

6. Next, picture a vibrant pastel shade of indigo descending all around you. Feel this colour awakening you to your inner spirit and harmonising all parts of your being. Sense it enveloping you and awakening your consciousness to God.

7. Let this colour slowly change into a pastel shade of violet and feel it permeating everything around you. Feel this colour coming down above your head, just outside of what would normally be your field of vision, pouring over the whole of your being. Breathe this colour in and know that within it you may find time to rest and soothe your body, mind, feelings and spirit in the loving presence of God. Know that this colour will restore and replenish your whole Self. Breathe in this presence and feel it all around you. Feel all that is good in life: peace, love, joy, light and beauty. Know that you are a pure manifestation of God; that God does not work against itself, but seeks to be whole and in harmony with all. Seek to find this higher Self and let it shine through and permeate your entire being. Stay with this feeling for a while and strengthen your contact with God.

8. Slowly become aware of your surroundings and collect your thoughts. Finish with a positive affirmation:

Today I awaken to God in all. I acknowledge God's power working in me, through me and around me. I am aware of the pure spirit within and allow its transforming goodness to permeate my whole being, bringing all of my life into harmony.

9. Awareness
Try not to dissipate the work you have achieved on awakening yourself to spiritual dimensions in too much mental or external chatter. Cultivate peace and have mastery over your thoughts. As you prepare and eat breakfast and other meals, be aware of what you are doing. Whenever possible, eat in silence. Be aware of external sounds as well as your own inner thoughts and emotions, but do this with an element of non-attachment. Build on the peace and strength you have found. Understand that it is not just the material substance of food that gives you energy: the thoughts you put behind it energises it. Be thankful

for it, know that it has grown on God's Earth and that God's creative energy is contained within it.

10. A guide to the day

Throughout the rest of the day, make a conscious effort to re-establish your contact with God. Be conscious of your thoughts and actions. Find time to be quiet in mind and body for a few minutes at different times of the day. Whenever possible, bring your attention back to your breathing and make a conscious effort to centre your thoughts and feelings. Living creatively means working towards a greater awareness of life, becoming more in harmony with all that is around us and anchoring ourselves more firmly in God's presence.

If at all possible, walk in the fresh air. Walk where there are trees, where there is Nature, in a park or forest. Look for God's presence in the growth of life around you. Realise that everything is alive in God and saturated in its Divinity, that you are a part of that Divinity and a part of Nature. As you do so, take a deep breath and feel your whole self being energised and harmonised by the vast ocean of life around you.

Take a spiritually uplifting book with you. Sit and read a passage or two. Then be still and quiet for a moment and know that all is well in God's presence. Use keywords such as 'peace', 'joy', 'love', 'acceptance', 'trust', 'let go', or a positive affirmation at different times in the day to help you keep that link with the spiritual element of existence. Say them frequently to yourself and feel their influence upon your consciousness. Choose your words carefully. What you feed into your consciousness will be reflected in your life. The mind draws towards itself the things with which it is in tune. Everything responds to you at your current level of understanding and awareness. For this reason you need to observe your thoughts, emotions and actions throughout the day and cultivate creative and skilful thinking, conduct and speech.

11. A guide to problems

If you encounter a problem, this exercise may help you to see it from a different angle. First, find time to be quiet, calm and still for a few moments. Check that your breathing is calm, rhythmic and relaxed. If it is not, practise the relaxation and breathing exercise mentioned earlier in this chapter and feel yourself becoming more peaceful. Now use the following affirmation, taking its full meaning into your consciousness:

Knowing that Spirit is the one power that governs all and that this harmonious power flows through me, I know of no limitation in my life and claim a life of infinite possibilities. I am a nonresistant instrument for truth, love and goodness.

As the infinite Spirit within me knows no boundaries, there is nothing that I cannot do, face or overcome. All is in harmony with my life. I am at peace with all that surrounds me. I see through all things and recognize the Divine's presence in the centre of all.

Do not at any time make affirmative statements about the particular problem you are facing. To do otherwise would mean underrating the power of the Spirit and give power to any problem you face. This does not mean that we should not explore our wounds, fears and negative emotions. Instead, we need to discover ways to understand, own and transform them.

12. A guide to the evening

Find time in the evening to be quiet and reflect upon your day. Look for any negative areas that need more attention. Ask yourself whether there is anything within you that you need to be more aware of. Is there anything on which you need to work or change? Is there something you need at this moment in time? Make a note and keep a journal of any thoughts. Be honest with yourself and use your journal to help you understand and know the way you work – physically, mentally, creatively, emotionally, psychically, mediumistically and spiritually.

Round off your day by reading a passage from a spiritually uplifting book. Follow it with the relaxation and breathing exercise and a period of prayer and meditation (see the chapters on these for guidance). Finish by sending out some healing thoughts to those whom you know need help and to the leaders of all nations to make peace with one another, to the animal and plant kingdom and to the world at large – including Mother Earth herself. Distant healing has a positive effect not only on those to whom you direct it, but also upon yourself. It helps strengthen your spiritual nature: your capacity to empathise and discover unity with others, to find and bring peace in the world and perform spontaneous acts of compassion.

When you retire for the night, thank God for your life and for all the good in your life.

*   *   *

The exercises suggested in this chapter and book will hopefully give you some guidance on centring your life in the spirit. We do not wish you to follow everything without question, but would prefer you to take on board only that which feels right for your unfoldment. We hope you will continue to search for and discover numerous beneficial ways of awakening to and unfolding your wondrous authentic spiritual nature and its connections with the spirit world and the sacredness of all. May the path you tread be blessed with love and wisdom and be full of eternal joy and peace.

Notes

1. John's Gospel, 1:1, *Holy Bible: New International Version, Hodder and Stoughton*, 1988 reprint, page 148.

2. Based around a meditation practice by Swami Shivapremananda, *A Guide to Meditation: Part 2*, Yoga and Health Magazine, April 1995, pages 29–31.

3. "The popular opinion that these yogic abilities are not part of the path to Self-realisation is demonstrably wrong ... they cannot be separated from the essentially organic and unitary structure of Yoga." George Feuerstein, *The Yoga-Sutras of Patanjali*, Inner Traditions International, 1989 reprint, pages 104–5.

4. A view expressed by C. G. Jung (also shared by William James), in James Fadiman and Robert Frager's *Personality and Personal Growth*, Harper Collins, 1994, 3rd edition, page 86.

5. Information about Thomas Young and the Trichromacy Theory are from *The Guinness Encyclopedia of the Living World*, Guinness Publishing, 1992, page 189.

6. Paragraph based on H. L. Cooke, *Painting Techniques of the Masters*, Watson Guptil, 1972, page 38.

7. H. L. Cooke, *Painting Techniques of the Masters*, Watson Guptil, 1972, page 39.

8. D. McMonagle, *Science: Basic Facts*, Harper Collins, 1992, pages 51–2.

9. The Swiss psychiatrist, Carl Jung, wrote much on coming to terms with the shadow side of our personality and balancing it with the light. In Psychosynthesis psychology the Italian psychiatrist, Roberto Assagioli, formulated ideas around three basic levels of ourselves (higher, middle and lower). Ancient yogic texts mention the three *gunas*, which can be described in the following ways: (a) Actions that create harmony, are responsible, balanced, mindful and pure, flow spontaneously and freely from our nature and connect with and consider others and the environment (*sattvic* actions); (b) Actions that are influenced by self-centred desires, which cause a strain on our relationships with others and the environment and arise from a belief in self-importance (*rajasic* actions); (c) Actions that are performed from a confused, unclear and unthought through state of mind, which are irresponsible, have little consideration for the outcome, cause offence and harm other people and life (*tamasic* actions).

10. Based on exercises sometimes used in Psychosynthesis workshops.

11. From a saying by the German mystic, Meister Eckhart (1260 – 1327 CE).

12. C. G. Jung, *Memories, Dreams, Reflections*, Fontana Press, 1983, page 205.

13. Robert E. Ornstein, *The Psychology of Consciousness*, Jonathan Cape, 1975, page 145.

Appendix 1
Dynamic Thought
Glyn Edwards

*T*hought is a dynamic living force. Some regard it as the most vital, subtle and important force that exists in the universe. Though thought may be described as subtle matter, it is in many ways as solid as stone. For though the physical frame may die, our thoughts go on resonating in the ether, because thought, like our spirit, never dies.

Much of what we see and know as real in human dimensions of life is a creation of thought. For instance, buildings are the products of the thoughts of architects, cars of designers and engineers, medicine of biochemists and art of artists. Realms of thought are equally as real, relatively, as the living and evolving physical universe in which we live.

Our thoughts take on the form of anything they contemplate. For example, when we think of an object, our mind changes and shapes itself into the form of that object. This is how we perceive, not just through sight or touch, but through the mind. It is the mind that directs the other senses and affects the auric field. If we observe some of the processes of our mind and thoughts we will notice many modifications continually arising. And as our thoughts change, so will our auric field. Some mediums are able to see the effects that different thoughts have on the aura and various potentials that a person has.

The roles of thought in unfoldment
We need to understand the value and practice of prayer, meditation and silence in order that we can steady, fix and empower our thoughts. This will affect and change certain energies within our body, mind and aura and bring balance to various levels of our being. This will attract the right things, spiritually as well as materially, into our life and unfoldment.

We should also realise that our thoughts will play a dominant role in our unfoldment. In this work the development of creative and healthy thinking will be called upon. Our thoughts will mould and shape not only our character, but also our auric energy. Thoughts from external sources also have an impact on our aura. We encounter this external influence almost every day, in all areas of our lives: in our environments, the people we meet and things we do. All these affect and colour our thoughts, states of being and aura.

We have the power to change and grow

If you think you are weak, then weak you will be. If you think you cannot do something, then you will not. Everything we see, feel, hear and touch is an expression of our thoughts. This can be understood by observing the shifts in our different moods. When we are happy, the world becomes a beautiful place and when we are sad, it is not. This does not mean that we cannot change our character and perceptions of life, because we can by reprogramming our thoughts. It is we who place the limitations upon ourselves.

In mediumistic unfoldment, as an awareness of the spirit world becomes more predominant, various spirit influences will be seen blending with our consciousness. Yet it is still our choice to what extent we allow this to happen, how much we open ourselves to the spirit's influence and embrace wider states of awareness. We see from this how important it is to know our thoughts, as through them we will attract corresponding influences. As we attract, so do we repel. This law of attraction and repulsion can be seen operating at various levels of our being.

Focusing the mind

Most of our thoughts are not well grounded and are random. But through reflection and meditation we can strengthen and clarify them. This will encourage our thoughts to settle down and to crystallise into definite shape. Through creative thinking, introspection and meditation we can reprogramme our minds. Through this we start to gain more mastery over our thoughts, which is an essential part of spiritual growth. By having more control over our thoughts we can become aware of different levels of our consciousness, and when we know how to apply our thoughts we can then enhance positive attitudes to life.

Applied thinking focuses the mind on an object of thought and sustained positive thought keeps the mind continually engaged in the act of creating; thus creating right attitudes towards ourselves, others and our environments. This enables us to discover right directions to take in life. It also helps focus our talents and potentials and creates a new environment in our mind, which enables us to receive and form thoughts that are inspiring and infused from levels beyond ourselves.

The power of the mind

By bringing the power of the mind behind prayer and meditation, we enable them to become more effective and creative tools. Everything we do begins in the mind. For us to bring the mind to exert its creative powers, the ability to focus our thoughts is obviously important.

In our spiritual unfoldment we are presumably hoping to bring about some movement in our consciousness so we can apprehend what lies beyond our senses of sight, hearing, touch, taste and smell and how non-physical realms interconnect with the physical world. This may happen spontaneously. Yet to develop our potential, we need to apply something more and focus our mind and thoughts in order to inspire sustained spontaneous awareness. By focussing our mind and thoughts we can bring this about.

Methods for internalising awareness

When we learn how to develop the concentrative powers of our mind, we find that when we meditate, or when communication of the spirit world is taking place, we are able to focus our awareness more firmly and deeply upon what we are doing. By learning how to gather our thoughts we can learn how to focus and steady them. The greatest impediment to concentration is restlessness and distraction. If we observe our mind and thoughts, we will see they have a natural tendency to wander. Often there is a never ending stream of connected and disconnected thoughts. Our minds also experience periods of dullness, forgetfulness and laziness.

Although we all have some ability to concentrate – without it we would be unable to complete any task – healthy sustained levels of concentration can only be achieved when we are relaxed and at one with our mental, physical and emotional selves. For many, concentration is impossible to sustain for any length of time, and trying to force the mind to concentrate can mean unhealthily suppressing much of what is going on at various levels of our personality. This is why it is important to understand and know ourselves, to learn about our thoughts, emotions and bodies and how they affect us. This is also why relaxation exercises before meditation are important. For if we cannot relax, we will not be able to meditate. Or in the case of mediumship, properly attune to the spirit world.

For spiritual unfoldment, our concentration needs to be developed to a certain degree. If we have an appreciable degree of concentration, we will be able to do and achieve more. To maintain spiritual progress we need to go beyond ordinary concentration, to levels where the mind and consciousness are brought in tune and influenced by our spiritual nature in order to bring about changes in the whole of our being.

But for many of us, our minds are only occasionally steady and truly focused. In spiritual unfoldment we are dealing with energies that are constantly fluctuating and displaying subtleties that our more regular states of mind misses or misinterprets, which also happens in mediumistic unfoldment. We will therefore need to learn how to interpret and observe the mind. We do this by becoming an inner spectator, sitting and observing the mind go through its mental activities, as though we were watching a film. As the mind begins to realise that we are not becoming involved with our thoughts, it begins to settle. It is at this point that we can introduce a word of spiritual significance or an attribute we wish to develop and allow our awareness to flow towards the meaning of the word.

If thoughts intrude we should not become disturbed or involved in them, but let them come and go and return to the object of our attention. We simply observe our thoughts and let them go without becoming anxious about or trying to suppress them. If emotions intrude, we follow the same principle: we simply watch them come and go. They will soon pass. But we ought not to attempt pushing them away, as it can cause problems of denial. A time will come when through this practice we will stay for longer in uninterrupted attention and we will be well on our way to mastering the art of concentration and wondrously empowering our thoughts and enriching our spiritual lives.

Appendix 2
Awakening to Creative Life
Santoshan

We stand in a unique position where we need to be involved in the making of a New Earth. Our current age calls us to embrace an inclusive, universal and creative spirituality; one that encompasses living the whole of our life as skilfully, peacefully and compassionately as possible. It involves manifesting qualities that lead to recognizing the profound unity we share with all people and Nature and the responsibilities this brings. This is more than just a mere knowing, but a state of being that is authentically lived.

This transforming aspect of spirituality is always there inviting us. It is an expression of supreme creativity that connects us with the powers of the universe, which can be manifested in each moment and called upon to enrich our world and daily interactions. Spirituality is in many ways about being awake to this potential, and the abilities and possibilities that are available to us at all times, which can lead us to being spontaneously creative and to participate skilfully in life as it unfolds.

An integral and creative approach to spirituality is multidimensional and acknowledges an array of levels and stages of unfoldment, without undermining insights of an essential oneness. Though it involves travelling through a multiple of spheres, such as a spirit world, a psychological world and an ecological world, it is a single integration that seeks interaction with the all-ness of healthy living. It is when we include the whole, including the natural world, that we open to a path that has been recognized by many traditions: one that is life affirming. It is a spirituality that links us with the beginning of creation, because of its connections with the creative force and mind that has pervaded the universe since its birth.

Deep within us we know intuitively that not only life on our planet, but also the universe has a profound interconnected intelligence and purpose. If we consider how our living universe came into being and how it is holistic, integral and forever in the process of evolving, we realise it is an important part of who we are, as we are all incredible products of the universe and its awe inspiring creativity.

Through awakening to these deeper dimensions of spirituality, we touch realms of experience that have been realised by many of the world's great mystics and seers and discover knowledge of the profound connections we share with the creativity of Earth, Nature, spirit and the cosmos. Although no two humans, snowflakes or blades of grass are identical, all connect with an underlying unity. All life possesses a unique spark of the Divine and its potential to create – to bring about harmony, balance and creative beauty into the world, which are essential facets of healthy spirituality.

When we create, we take part in and celebrate the creativity that exists within our universe. We in fact already possess all that we need to be in a productive interactive relationship with the Divine's creativity in the cosmos; we only have to find the intuitive insight that is called for to overcome the appearance of separation from it. When we do this, we open ourselves to the evolving and transforming power of an active spirituality.

Yet past conditioning makes unfoldment difficult. We see ourselves as physically separate. Our senses create the appearance of being singular and set apart from other people, objects and life around us, which leads to self-centred actions. Yet not only do the Buddha's and many of the world's great teachings tell us that this is a wrong perception, but quantum physics has also discovered this to be true.

It is when we are at one with the spiritual core of our being that life starts to speak to us in fresh and dynamic ways that are not tied to conditioned perceptions. A healthy way forward involves interacting with numerous areas of growth, which include acquiring an Earth/ Nature-centric vision, awakening to inclusive realms of spirituality and growing beyond the boundaries that separate us. This enlarges who we are and leads us to previously unrecognized potential, to discover new realms of possibility and move beyond restrictive patterns, to realise that change and growth are always possible.

This is a spirituality that embraces and acts upon wisdom that crosses all boundaries in order to include all – to see all as an interrelated and unified sacred whole, with profound meaning and purpose – which, if we are open enough to take part in it, can enrich and transform our lives in every moment.

The search is always ongoing and involves being open to new discoveries and the problems of contemporary living, to learning how to tread lightly upon the Earth, live peacefully and purify our minds, hearts and awareness and perform creative acts that are in harmony with the natural world and others. The creative impulse within us takes on deeper meaning when our actions are performed as expressions of spiritual living and a recognition of our unity with all – with both human and non-human life.

Gaia consciousness

A particular form of creative and Nature centred spirituality has been promoted in the last three decades by the author and teacher Matthew Fox, as a key element of many important mystical and spiritual teachings. It places strong emphasis on original blessing/goodness. The term 'creation centred spirituality' was suggested as a name for this creative and mystical branch of spirituality in the late 1960s by Fox's college mentor, Pere Chenu. GreenSpirit is a UK based version of creation spirituality ideals, with members from around the globe. It honours Nature as a great teacher, the interconnected sacredness of all life, affirms differences and the prophetic voice of artists.

Many members of GreenSpirit trace their roots back to the cosmological wisdom of the early eastern mystics and medieval Christians, such as Hildegard of Bingen and Francis of Assisi, and embrace the Earth as an integral part of spirituality. This strongly Nature centered spirituality finds common ground with indigenous beliefs and practices, such as shamanism, middle and far eastern spiritualities and contemporary science. All people and traditions, *no matter what faith*, are valued and respected.

It affirms diversity and seeks wholeness and unity between male and female, homosexual, bisexual and heterosexual, different races, cultures and religions, Earth, the world of Nature – with its essential psychic and creative forces – and humans, who are after all a part of Nature. It has deep connections with the intuitive, creative, caring and compassionate elements of spirituality.

*　　*　　*

Note. This is a changed Appendix to one that originally appeared in the first edition of this book. The first part was written as an article for the Watkins Review to coincide with the release of *Spirituality Unveiled: Awakening to Creative Life*. For more information about the book, visit www.spiritualityunveiled.com. For information about GreenSpirit, to join their social network, become a member and receive their magazine, see details below. To join the free worldwide social network of Creation Spirituality Communities, visit originalblessing.ning.com.

Spirituality Unveiled:
Awakening to Creative Life
Santoshan
Earth Books
ISBN 978-1-84694-509-0
144 pages

GreenSpirit
www.greenspirit.org.uk

Recommended Reading

Mediumistic Unfoldment

Harry Boddington, *Materialisations*, Spiritual Truth Press.

Harry Boddington, *University of Spiritualism*, Psychic Press.

Glyn Edwards, *The Potential of Mediumship: A Collection of Essential Teachings and Exercises*, S. Wollaston.

Harry Edwards, *A Guide for the Development of Mediumship*, Con-Psy Publications.

J. J. Morse, *Practical Occultism*, Branden Press.

Ursula Roberts, *All About Mediumship*, Two Worlds Publishing.

Santoshan, with conversations with Glyn Edwards, *Realms of Wondrous Gifts: Psychic, Mediumistic and Miraculous Powers in the Great Wisdom Traditions*, The Gordon Higginson Fellowship.

Psychical Research and the Hidden Potential in Humankind

Paul Beard, *Survival of Death*, Pilgrim Books.

Nona Coxhead, *Mind Power*, Mandala.

Brian Inglis, *Science and Parascience: A History of the Paranormal, 1914–1939*, Hodder and Stoughton.

Raynor C. Johnson, *The Imprisoned Splendour*, Hodder and Stoughton.

David Lorimer, *Whole in One: The Near Death Experience and the Ethic of Interconnectedness*, Arkana.

Archie Roy, *The Archives of the Mind*, SNU Publications.

Herbert Thurston, *The Physical Phenomena of Mysticism*, Roman Catholic Books.

Spiritual Unfoldment

Glyn Edwards and Santoshan, *Spirit Gems: Essential Guidance for Spiritual, Mediumistic and Creative Unfoldment* (revised and expanded edition of *Unleash your Spiritual Power and Grow*), S. Wollaston.

Ursular King, *The Search for Spirituality: Our Global Quest for Meaning and Fulfilment*, Canterbury Press.

Jack Kornfield, *After the Ecstasy, the Laundry: How the Heart Grows Wise on the Spiritual Path*, Rider.

Jack Kornfield, *A Path with Heart: A guide through the Perils and Promises of Spiritual Life*, Rider.

Ursula Roberts, *Hints on Spiritual Unfoldment*, Psychic Press.

Wayne Teasdale, *The Mystic Heart: Discovering a Universal Spirituality in the World's Religions*, New World Library.

Creative, Nature and Gaia Conscious Spirituality

Thomas Berry, *Dream of the Earth*, Sierra Club Books.

Deepak Chopra, *Power, Freedom and Grace: Living from the Source of Lasting Happiness*, Amber-Allen Publishing.

Chris Clarke, *Weaving the Cosmos: Science, Religion and Ecology*, Earth Books.

Matthew Fox, *Original Blessing: A Primer in Creation Spirituality*, Tarcher/Putnam.

Joyce and Rive Higginbotham, *Paganism: An Introduction to Earth-Centred Religions*, Llewellyn Publications.

Marian Van Eyk McCain (compiled and edited by), *GreeenSpirit: Path to a New Consciousness*, Earth Books.

John O'Donohue, *Anam Cara: The Spiritual Wisdom from the Celtic World*, Transworld.

Santoshan (Stephen Wollaston), *Spirituality Unveiled: Awakening to Creative Life*, Earth Books.

Yogic Wisdom

TKV Desikachar, *Reflections on Yoga Sutras of Patanjali*, Krishnamacharya Yoga Mandiram.

Swami Dharmananda and Santoshan, *The House of Wisdom: Yoga Spirituality of the East and West*, Mantra Books.

Eknath Easwaran (translation by), *The Bhagavad Gita*, Shambhala.

Georg Feuerstein, *The Shambhala Guide to Yoga*, Shambhala.

Alan Jacobs, *The Principal Upanishads: A Poetic Translation*, Mantra Books.

M. P. Pandit, *The Yoga of Self-perfection: Talks Based on Sri Aurobindo's Synthesis of Yoga*, Dipti.

Swami Satyananda Saraswati, *A Systematic Course in the Ancient Tantric Techniques of Yoga and Kriya*, Yoga Publications Trust.

Swami Shankarananda, *Consciousness is Everything: The Yoga of Kashmir Shaivism*, Shaktipat.

Buddhist Wisdom

Ajahn Chah, *Food for the Heart: The Collected Teachings of Ajan Chah*, Wisdom.

Thich Nhat Hanh, *The Heart of the Buddha's Teaching: Transforming Suffering into Peace, Joy and Liberation – the Four Noble Truths, the Noble Eightfold Path and other Basic Buddhist Teachings*, Parallax.

The Ven. Balangoda Ananda Maitreya (translation by), *The Dhammapada: The Path of Truth* (revised by Rose Kramer), Parallax.

Nyanaponika Thera, *The Vision of the Dhamma*, Buddhist Publication Society.

Tarthang Tulku, *Gestures of Balance: A Guide to Awareness, Self-healing and Meditation*, Dharma Publishing.

Christian Wisdom

Cynthia Bourgeault, *The Wisdom Jesus: Transforming Heart and Mind*, Shambhala.

Bede Griffiths, *The One Light: Bede Griffiths Principal Writings* (edited with a commentary by Bruno Barnhart), Templegate.

Karen King, *The Gospel of Mary Madgala*, Polebridge Press.

John Main, *Essential Writings* (selected with an introduction by Laurence Freeman), Orbis Books.

John R. Mabry, *The Way of Thomas: Nine Insights for Enlightened Living from the Secret Sayings of Jesus*, Circle Books.

Elaine Pagels, *The Gnostic Gospels*, Vintage.

Brian C. Taylor, *Becoming Human: Core Teachings of Jesus*, Cowley Publications.

Pierre Teilhard de Chardin, *Pierre Teilhard de Chardin* (writings selected with an introduction by Ursula King), Orbis Books.

Jewish Wisdom

Ellen Bernstein, *The Splendor of Creation, A Biblical Ecology*, Cleveland, The Pilgrim Press.

David A Cooper, *Essential Kabbalah*, Sounds True.

Michael Lerner, *Spirit Matters,* Hampton Roads.

Sufi Wisdom

James Fadiman and Robert Frager (editors), *Essential Sufism*, Castle.

Reshad Feild, *Steps to Freedom: Discources on the Essential Knowledge of the Heart*, Chalice Guild.

Seyyed Hossein Nasr, *The Garden of Truth: The Vision and Promise of Sufism, Islam's Mystical Tradition*, Harper One.

New Thought

Raymond Charles Barker, *You Are Invisible*, DeVorss.

Roy Eugene Davis, *Studies in Truth*, CSA Press.

Joel S. Goldsmith, *Practising the Presence*, Fowler.

Ernest Holmes, *The Science of Mind*, Putnam.

Ernest Holmes, *This Thing Called You*, Putnam.

Ralph Waldo Trine, *In Tune with the Infinite*, Mandala.

Methods of Meditation

Thomas Berry, with additional material by Brian Swimme (selected by June
   Raymond), *Meditations with Thomas Berry*, GreenSpirit.

Roy Eugene Davis, *An Easy Guide to Meditation*, CSA Press.

Venerable Henepola Gunaratana, *Mindfulness in Plain English*, Wisdom.

Peter Ng (edited by), *The Hunger for Depth and Meaning: Learning to Meditate with
   John Main*, Medio Media.

Stephen Levine, *A Gradual Awakening*, Gateway.

John Novak, *How to Meditate*, Crystal Clarity.

Reginald A Ray, *Touching Enlightenment: Finding Realization in the Body*, Sounds True.

Methods of Prayer

M.V. Dunlop, *Contemplative Meditation*, Fellowship of Meditation.

Sam Hamilton-Poore, *Earth Gospel: A Guide to Prayer for God's Creation*, Upper
   Room Books.

Thomas Keating, *Open Mind, Open Heart: The Contemplative Dimension of the
   Gospel*, Continuum.

Thomas Merton, *New Seeds of Contemplation*, Shambhala.

Henri J. M. Nouwen, *The Only Necessary Things: Living a Prayerful Life* (compiled
   and edited by Wendy Greer), Darton, Longman and Todd.

Alan Walker, *Prayer for Everyday Living*, Bounty Books.

Mantra

Swami Vishnu Devananda, *Meditation and Mantras*, Om Lotus.

Eknath Easwaran, *The Unstruck Bell*, Nilgiri.

Swami Sivananda Radha, *Mantras: Words of Power*, Timeless Books.

Pandit Rajmani Tigunait, *The Power of Mantra and the Mystery of Initiation*, Yoga
   International Books.

Facing and Overcoming Illness and Caring for the Dying

Elisabeth Kübler-Ross, *On Death and Dying: What the Dying have to Teach Doctors, Nurses, Clergy and their own Families*, Collier.

Stephen Levine, *Who Dies? An Investigation of Conscious Living and Conscious Dying*, Gateway.

Sogyal Rinpoche, *The Tibetan Book of Living and Dying*, Rider.

Transpersonal Psychology and Integral Wisdom

Roberto Assagioli, *Psychosynthesis: A Manual of Principles and Techniques*, Aquarian.

Christina Grof and Stanislav Grof, *The Stormy Search for the Self: Understanding and Living with Spiritual Emergency*, Thorsons.

Brant Cortright, *Integral Psychology: Yoga, Growth, and Opening the Heart*, SUNY.

Theadore Roszak, *The Voice of the Earth: An Exploration of Ecopsychology*, Phanes.

John Welwood, *Towards a Psychology of Awakening: Buddhism, Psychotherapy, and the Path of Personal and Spiritual Transformation*, Shambhala.

Ken Wilber, *The Integral Vision: A Very Short Introduction to the Revolutionary Integral Approach to Life, God, the Universe, and Everything*, Shambhala.

Biographies

Shirley Du Boulay, *Beyond the Darkness: Biography of Bede Griffiths*, Circle Books.

Gordon Higginson (compiled by Jean Bassett), *On the Other Side of Angels*, SNU Publication.

Paramahansa Yogananda, *Autobiography of a Yogi*, Self-Realization Fellowship.

GreenSpirit Book Series (first four titles in the low-cost series)

Marian Van Eyk McCain (compiled and edited by), *What is Green Spirituality?*

Marian Van Eyk McCain (compiled and edited by), *All Our Relations: Connections with the More-Than-Human World*.

Greg Morter and Niamh Brennan, *The Universe Story: In Science and Myth*.

Santoshan (Stephen Wollaston), *Rivers of Green Wisdom: Exploring Christian and Yogic Earth Centred Spirituality*.

*   *   *

THE POTENTIAL OF MEDIUMSHIP
A Collection of Essential Teachings and Exercises
(expanded edition)
Glyn Edwards
Compiled and with an introduction by Santoshan

Presents an inspiring collection of teachings, along with numerous essential exercises for unfolding mediumistic and spiritual gifts. In this first ever anthology of Glyn Edwards' wisdom, he shared first-hand accounts about his own mediumistic experiences and imparted profound insights that will help you to move forward with your abilities. There are chapters here for beginners and the more advanced that reveal how the spirit world can communicate with and work through us and prove survival of life after death.

128 page expanded edition
ISBN 978-0-9569210-3-1

eBook edition available from Smashwords:
www.smashwords.com

'There should be many more books like this!'
– Psychic News.

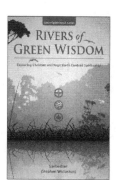

RIVERS OF GREEN WISDOM
Exploring Christian and Yogic
Earth Centred Spirituality
Santoshan (Stephen Wollaston)

In *Rivers of Green Wisdom* the author shares personal reflections on Christian, Yogic and Earth centred wisdom, and unveils central teachings about the sacredness of Nature. The book covers both past and present understanding about our interdependent relationship with the natural world and how various teachers have looked for east-west fusions for deeper and more responsible living.

86 pages
ISBN 978-0-9935983-2-6

Low-cost printed and eBook editions available. For more details visit www.greenspirit.org.uk

'Seldom do you find such practised clarity in revealing the wisdom of Spirit.'
– Sky McCain, Vedantist and author of
Planet as Self: An Earthen Spirituality.

128 pages
ISBN 978-0-9569210-1-7

SPIRIT GEMS
Essential Guidance for Spiritual, Mediumistic and Creative Unfoldment
Glyn Edwards and Santoshan

Spirit Gems is a revised and expanded edition of the authors' second book, which provides practical steps for discovering how to live more freely, deeply and peacefully. Glyn Edwards and Santoshan write beautifully whilst covering essentials such as living in the now, facing our fears, finding unity with all and harmonising the whole of ourselves. Both authors share profound insights for immersing our lives in spiritually and mediumistically centred living. Let their wisdom take you on a journey through various levels of your individual self to ever-present realms of the spirit.

'A must for anyone's bookshelf.'
– The Greater World Newsletter.
Review of first edition.

144 pages
ISBN 978-1-84694-509-0

SPIRITUALITY UNVEILED
Awakening to Creative Life
Santoshan (Stephen Wollaston)
Foreword by Ian Mowll

Spirituality Unveiled puts forward a succinct and compelling synthesis of numerous spiritual traditions. Whilst weaving together insights from contemporary and past masters of spirituality, along with holistic and Earth centred wisdom, it beautifully highlights teachings about the essentials of creative unfoldment. *Spirituality Unveiled* invites readers to join in the important search to find a healthy interaction with life. Key areas include the power of creativity and harmonious living with the natural world.

'Integral thinking at its best ... a masterful synthesis.'
– Marian Van Eyk McCain, editor of
GreenSpirit: Path to a New Consciousness.

REALMS OF WONDROUS GIFTS

Psychic, Mediumistic and Miraculous Powers in the Great Mystical and Wisdom Traditions

Santoshan, with conversations with Glyn Edwards

An in-depth look at psychic, mediumistic and miraculous powers in the world's great mystical and wisdom traditions. Includes two extensive sections with Glyn Edwards.

FREE eBook
ISBN 978-1-4657-6671-7
www.smashwords.com

'A rare and enriching book.'
– Eileen Davies, internationally renowned medium and spiritual teacher.

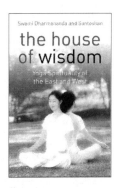

THE HOUSE OF WISDOM

Yoga Spirituality of the East and West

Swami Dharmananda and Santoshan

Foreword by Glyn Edwards

Draws on a variety of spiritual paths to encourage wiseful living today.

'An excellent book ... a real treasure-house of spiritual knowledge.'
– Julie Friedeberger, author of
The Healing Power of Yoga.

224 pages
ISBN 978-1-846940-24-8

AUDIO CDs BY AND DOWNLOADS OF GLYN EDWARDS

**Audio CDs by Glyn Edwards available from
the Mind-Body-Spirit Online website:**
www.mindbodyspiritonline.co.uk
Tel: (01202) 267684 (outside UK: +441202 267684)

Downloads of CDs by Glyn Edwards available from:
www.listening2spirit.com